Routledge Revivals

Rape on Trial

First published in 1987, *Rape on Trial* investigates the impact of the Sexual Offences (Amendment) Act, 1976 and considers the treatment of rape victims by the courts in United Kingdom. Extracts from trials are used extensively, and the author examines in particular: how the anonymity provisions have worked out in practice; how far the victim's previous sexual history is brought up in court; how far she is held to be responsible for her victimisation; ways in which the validity of her complaint is questioned in court; and defence strategies to present her as a legitimate victim. Also included are a critical discussion of the controversial question of sentencing for rape, and new proposals for legislative and procedural change. Extremely pertinent to current times, this book will be of interest to students of law, criminology, sociology as well as to any concerned citizen.

Rape on Trial

Zsuzsanna Adler

Routledge
Taylor & Francis Group

First published in 1987
by Routledge & Kegan Paul

This edition first published in 2022 by Routledge
4 Park Square, Milton Park, Abingdon, Oxon, OX14 4RN
and by Routledge
605 Third Avenue, New York, NY 10017

Routledge is an imprint of the Taylor & Francis Group, an informa business

Publisher's Note
The publisher has gone to great lengths to ensure the quality of this reprint but points out that some imperfections in the original copies may be apparent.

Disclaimer
The publisher has made every effort to trace copyright holders and welcomes correspondence from those they have been unable to contact.

A Library of Congress record exists under ISBN: 0710208049

ISBN: 978-1-032-33218-5 (hbk)
ISBN: 978-1-003-31916-0 (ebk)
ISBN: 978-1-032-33333-5 (pbk)

Book DOI 10.4324/9781003319160

RAPE
ON TRIAL

RAPE
ON TRIAL

ZSUZSANNA ADLER

Routledge & Kegan Paul
London and New York

First published in 1987 by
Routledge & Kegan Paul Ltd
11 New Fetter Lane, London EC4P 4EE

Published in the USA by
Routledge & Kegan Paul Inc.
in association with Methuen Inc.
29 West 35th Street, New York, NY 10001

Set in Ehrhardt, 11 on 12 pt
and printed in Great Britain
by Butler & Tanner Ltd,
Frome, Somerset

Library of Congress Cataloging in Publication Data

Adler, Zsuzsanna.
  Rape on trial.
  Bibliography: p.
  Includes index.
  1. Rape—Great Britain. I. Title.
KD7976.R3A27 1987   345.41'02532   86–15586
                        344.1052532

British Library CIP Data also available
ISBN 0–7102–0804–9

Contents

Acknowledgments

This book is based on research undertaken for a Ph.D. thesis at Bedford College, University of London. It would have been impossible to carry out the study without the cooperation of the Central Criminal Court, and I am particularly grateful to the Court Administrator for allowing me to attend trials, and to the staff of the Listing Office.

I owe special gratitude to Professor Lord McGregor, my supervisor, who gave unfailing guidance and advice at all stages of the study. Many other colleagues and friends, both at Bedford College and elsewhere, were helpful in discussing various aspects of the work and offering new insights. Particular thanks are due to Pamala Klein, Colin Tapper and Selina Salisbury for their valuable comments on the manuscript, and to Peter Nathan for his part in introducing me to criminal law and procedure.

Last, but by no means least, I would like to thank Jessica, Adam and Christopher for tolerance well beyond their years; and John, without whose encouragement and support this book might not have seen the light of day.

Introduction

A new law on rape, the Sexual Offences (Amendment) Act, was passed in 1976. Its main purpose was to make it less of an ordeal for victims to report rape and to give evidence at the trial. In particular, it gives anonymity to women reporting rape and restricts the scope of cross-examination about their sexual past during the trial. The study on which this book is based set out to examine the impact of law reform in this area, with particular emphasis on the experience of rape victims, on the basis of a series of rape trials conducted at the Central Criminal Court.

Chapter 1 examines some of the main problems involved in the dealings of the criminal justice system with the crime of rape, and examines common stereotypes and misconceptions about the nature of the offence. The physical and psychological impact of rape on its victims is also considered, as are changing attitudes towards the victim and her plight in recent years. Chapter 2 outlines the early development of rape law and discusses its impact on current thinking and policy making in this area. The background of the appointment of the Advisory Group on the Law of Rape, on whose recommendations the 1976 legislation was based, is also considered. Chapter 3 introduces the Central Criminal Court and its judges and explains how the research was carried out. The trial process is briefly outlined, and the trials, defendants and victims are described.

Chapters 4 to 8 deal with the substantive findings of the study, and rely extensively on verbatim extracts from the trials. Chapter 4 considers the question of anonymity, for both defendants and victims, and draws attention to various problems that have arisen in implementing the relevant provision. Chapter 5 discusses the type of sexual history evidence that had been brought up at trials before the 1976 Act, and contrasts these with post-1976 developments. In particular, it examines the way in which judges have interpreted the new legislation, and points to areas where the law's practical implementation falls short of the aims and intentions of Parliament. Chapter 6 discusses the victim's previous sexual relationship with the defendant, and how far evidence of that is brought up in court. In addition, it indicates how indirect evidence, innuendo and suggestion, all outside the scope of the 1976 legislation, are used to discredit the victim's sexual character. Chapter 7 looks at other attributes of rape victims which also tend to become central foci of rape trials, such as their general reputation or any perceived contributory behaviour on their part. The extent to which these and similar factors appear to influence the decision-making of juries is also discussed. Chapter 8 considers the outcome of trials, the mitigation and sentencing process, and examines how far these parallel the trial process. It examines the extent to which the severity of the offence as well as the length of sentence are determined with reference to stereotypical views of the offence.

Chapter 9 considers legislative reform in other jurisdictions, in an attempt to put the English experience in a broader international context. It argues that there are lessons to be learnt from current trends in overseas law reform, some of which has met with considerably more success than has the 1976 legislation in this country.

Finally, Chapter 10 puts forward a number of suggestions, both for substantive law reform and procedural change, which may bring about genuine improvement in the way in which rape victims are treated by the courts. These suggestions for change have been formulated in the light of the findings of this study, and of the Criminal Law Revision Committee's 1984 Report on Sexual Offences.

Chapter 1

The trouble with rape

The last decade has witnessed considerable public concern over the way in which rape cases are handled when they get to the courts. Criticism began in earnest in 1975 with the controversial and widely debated decision of the House of Lords in the case of Morgan,[1] a decision which the popular media labelled a 'Rapist's Charter'. The crux of that judgment was that a man cannot be convicted of rape if he genuinely believed that the woman was consenting to sexual intercourse, however fanciful and unreasonable the grounds for his belief. This caused a substantial uproar, and much anxiety was expressed as to how easy it would be in future for men to get away with rape. In the wake of the controversy, the Home Secretary appointed an Advisory Group on the Law of Rape, whose Report[2] reaffirmed the Morgan ruling, and recommended a number of important changes in the law. These were incorporated in the Sexual Offences (Amendment) Act 1976[3] and there were high hopes that the new legislation would give the rape victim a considerably better deal in court. But rape regularly returns to serious public attention as a result of particularly inept judicial handling of various widely reported cases.

The Morgan controversy was quickly followed by a political and media outcry over a six-month suspended sentence passed on a youth who had pleaded guilty to raping two women at knifepoint. The furore over that case was exceeded in the so-called 'guardsman' case, in which the Court of Appeal, to the vocal outrage of MPs and feminist groups, suspended a three-year prison sentence passed on a young man convicted of a serious indecent assault and grievous bodily harm because of the damage imprisonment might do to his promising army career.

Then there was the Glasgow case, where the authorities refused to prosecute in a particularly vicious multiple rape, and which led to the resignation of Mr Nicholas Fairbairn as Solicitor General of Scotland. The victim herself eventually brought a private prosecution against a number of youths, one of whom was sentenced to twelve years' imprisonment.

Controversy was renewed when, in January 1982, Judge Richards at Ipswich Crown Court imposed a fine on a man convicted of rape because he felt that his victim, a hitchhiker, was also to blame and that this mitigated the seriousness of the offence. The judge said the case was a tragedy for the defendant, a father of two who had no previous record of sexual offences. Although he conceded that a woman hitching home late at night should be protected by the law, he found this victim guilty of a great deal of 'contributory negligence'. In fact, the concept of contributory negligence is not part of any branch of the criminal law. Furthermore, while a handful of offenders each year receive a non-custodial sentence, a fine is definitely not in line with the general level of sentencing for this offence. Nevertheless, Judge Richards' comments received hearty support from Sir Melford Stevenson, a retired High Court Judge, who went on record as saying that 'it is the height of imprudence for any girl to hitchhike at night. That is so plain, it isn't really worth stating. She is in the true sense asking for it.'[4] Few would disagree that it is imprudent for anyone, irrespective of sex, to expose themselves unnecessarily to the risk of muggings and assaults of any kind. But the arguments used by these judges go far beyond the statement of this precautionary view. They single out the victim of rape and suggest that imprudent behaviour on her part excuses, or at least strongly mitigates, the conduct of the offender. The Lord Chancellor repudiated Judge Richards' remarks, and the Lord Chief Justice subsequently ruled that rape should be punished by immediate imprisonment, except in 'wholly exceptional circumstances'.[5]

At the end of the same year, Judge Price at Leeds Crown Court imposed a twelve-month prison sentence, with eight months suspended, on a man convicted of raping a 6-year-old girl. Taking into account two months in prison on remand, and time off for good behaviour, the man only served twenty-five days after his conviction. The Prime Minister took the unusual step of aligning herself in the Commons with those who regarded this sentence as 'totally incomprehensible'. Within days, it was announced that rape would in future only be tried by the most senior judges. As Zander noted,

Mrs Thatcher was yesterday getting political credit for the new directive that only the most senior judges qualified to take murder cases will in future be able to take rape cases. But it seems that the initiative for the change came not from her but from the Lord Chancellor who was heartily fed up with the way he repeatedly found himself dealing with bizarre decisions of maverick circuit judges in these sensitive cases.[6]

In fact promoting rape to the category of murder for trial purposes is unlikely to have much impact, as most rape cases were already being tried by the most senior judges before this directive. Besides, there is no evidence that seniority makes for greater sensitivity to the plight of the rape victim, or indeed for heavier sentencing. It is much more likely that differences in sentencing reflect individual idiosyncracies rather than status in the judicial hierarchy.

In any event, the bizarre decisions and pronouncements continue. Just a month later, a judge at Cambridge was reported to have directed a jury that women sometimes say 'no' when they mean 'yes', and to remember the expression 'stop it I like it'. In December 1983, an Old Bailey judge, commenting on a man who had had intercourse with a friend's 7-year-old daughter, said that this struck him as 'being one of the kind of accidents that could almost happen to anyone'. In May 1985, a magistrate remarked that the rape of a prostitute was 'an odd thing – it is like a contradiction in terms'. The catalogue of judicial *faux pas*, indicating gross and irremediable insensitivity on the part of individual judges, is almost endless.

But there are other indications too that all is not well with the law of rape. First, rape is a very much underreported offence, and some feel that this, 'more than anything serves as an example of the appalling inability of the criminal justice system to deal with the problem'.[7] The Home Office recognises that criminal statistics do not reveal the total amount of crime committed, and that offences recorded by the police represent only a proportion, possibly a small proportion, of crimes actually committed. North American studies suggest that between one in ten and one in twenty-five victims report sexual assaults to the police,[8] and there are strong indications in this country too that a significant number of rapes do not come to the attention of the authorities. The London Rape Crisis Centre reports that only a quarter of the women who contact them report to the police, a proportion which has been constant over the years since they started operating in 1976.[9] It must be remembered, of course, that not all victims contact Rape Crisis Centres either, and that the true level of underreporting may be very much higher than this figure suggests. Nevertheless, it is comparable to the findings of a recent London study which aimed to collect information about incidents of sexual assault, including rape, experienced by a group of women at any time in their lives.[10] Of the incidents identified in the sample, a quarter had been reported to the police. It is also noteworthy that almost half of the reported incidents involved victims under the age of 16, and that most of the rest involved assailants who were strangers. The recently published findings of the London inquiry into rape and sexual assault suggests that as little as 8 per cent of rapes may come to the attention of the police.[11] This discrepancy between the findings of various studies probably reflects differences in the samples used, but whatever the precise figures, they all suggest that an alarming proportion of rapes never come to light.

There are a number of reasons why women may choose not to invoke the authorities when they have been raped. They may be too upset even to consider reporting, or too embarrassed at the prospect of discussing intimate details of the incident with a stranger. Many women do not want anyone at all to know what they have been through. They may have been threatened by the assailant, and their fear of retaliation may deter them from going to the police. They may also be anxious about the reactions of the police. The screening of an episode of the BBC *Police* series in January 1982, which showed the highly insensitive interrogation of a victim by male police officers, will have done nothing to reassure women on that score. As the *Guardian* commented,

It was worse than one had feared ... it was not the language, nor even the unmitigated toughness that shocked ... [it was] the low-key brutality of the questioning – how many times had she had sex, when was the last time, did she menstruate properly, had she had psychiatric treatment.[12]

The case confirmed widespread suspicions that police attitudes are often unnecessarily harsh and hostile, and that consequently many victims are deterred from making formal complaints of rape. Although it should be pointed out that a number of police forces are trying to improve their investigative techniques and to treat rape complainants with more tact and sympathy than previously, women may still be frightened of encountering the attitudes and hostility described by one victim who did go to the police after being raped by an intruder in the middle of the night:

This woman said she had been in the force for seven years, and not once had she come across a genuine rape case. We get a lot of people who claim to have been raped [she said], girls who hitchhike and ask for trouble and then are surprised when they get it, or girlfriends who have rows or wives who have rows with their boyfriends or husbands, and think that maybe a rape claim would be a way of getting even with them. ... They asked where I lived and so on, I said I lived alone and one of the policemen said, well, what do you expect, an attractive girl like you living on your own. I was asked if I had fought back, and I'd said no, because he had a knife, and one of the policemen there said did you see the knife. And I realised that I hadn't seen the knife, and the policeman said well he probably didn't have one, he was just trying to frighten you. ... And the questions then went on to well, who have you been seeing, having sexual relations with, is there someone you've been leading on. The questioning was very much in terms of what had I done to make somebody treat me in this way.[13]

In spite of such deterrents to reporting, the yearly number of rapes and attempted rapes known to the police doubled between 1964 and 1974, and, with minor yearly fluctuations, the trend has been one of steady increase ever since.[14] In 1984, the latest year for which figures are available at the time of writing, 1,433 rape offences were recorded in England and Wales. However, a complaint to the police does not automatically figure in official statistics: crimes are only recorded if the police decide that there is prima facie evidence that the law has been broken. There is no way of establishing how many rape complaints do not receive a crime report at all, but the processing of recorded incidents is revealing. A recent study in Scotland[15] analysed the outcome of 196 reported incidents of sexual assault on the basis of police records and of the procurator fiscal's papers. Twenty-two per cent of the complaints were eventually classified as 'no crime', and this rate for sexual assault is very much higher than that found by studies on crime in general.

A little over two-thirds of recorded rape offences are cleared up by the police. Broadly speaking, an offence is classified as 'cleared up' if someone has been charged, summoned or cautioned for it. It is also said to be cleared up when the case is not proceeded with for various reasons, even though there is enough evidence for a charge to be made. The rate for rape has remained fairly constant over recent years, as well as consistently lower than that for other serious offences. In 1984, for example, the only notifiable sexual offence with a lower clear-up rate than rape (68 per cent) was indecent assault against a female at 58 per cent. By contrast, 89 per cent of assaults and 91 per cent of homicides were cleared up in the same year.

The majority of people (89 per cent in 1984) appearing before Magistrates' Courts on a rape charge are committed for trial to Crown Courts. Of the remainder, 89 per cent were discharged, or had their case withdrawn or dismissed, and 11 per cent were convicted of a rape offence.

The number of persons actually tried for rape offences at Crown Courts falls far behind the number reported to the police as having allegedly committed the offence. Somewhere around 40 per cent of the rapes recorded by the police are actually tried at a Crown Court, and this proportion has been steady for years. The conviction rate for rape is also consistently lower than that for other serious offences: 72 per cent of accused persons were convicted in 1984. When those pleading guilty are excluded, the conviction rate drops to below 50 per cent.[16]

It is not clear how far the low overall conviction rate for rape offences is a reflection of the fact that persons accused of rape are less likely to plead guilty than those accused of other serious offences. Figures relating to the relative proportion of guilty and not guilty pleas have only been published for one year in 1976, but they are revealing. Sixty per cent of those tried for rape offences pleaded 'not guilty'. The corresponding figures for other serious offences are significantly lower at 34 per cent for homicide, 28 per cent for all sexual offences, and 12 per cent for burglary. One is tempted to conclude that offenders and their legal advisers are well aware of the fact that they are more likely to get away with rape than with many other crimes.

As for sentence, the vast majority of persons convicted are

sentenced to an immediate custodial sentence, whether it is imprisonment, borstal or youth custody. The average length of imprisonment has been very steady over the years. The largest group, around a quarter of those imprisoned each year, receive sentences of between two and three years. The yearly number of offenders receiving life sentences has to date never exceeded fifteen.

Thus, as Figure 1.1 shows, the number of persons tried, let alone convicted, lags a long way behind the number of rape offences known by the police, which in all probability form only a small proportion of rapes committed in any case. The outcome of legal proceedings for rape hardly matches the seriousness with which the offence is generally regarded.

Yet, at the same time, rape is held to be one of the most serious crimes there is, as illustrated by the amount of media coverage accorded to the occasional mass rapist who catches the imagination of the public. The Cambridge rapist and, more recently, the romantically named Fox are examples of such offenders. While they are at large, stories of their latest act, interviews with their victims, and accounts of police efforts to catch them fill the columns until they are finally captured and tried. Rapes of this sort evoke a good deal of horror, indignation and fear, particularly in the communities where they occur. Police efforts to catch the man are stepped up, women organise demonstrations and protest marches, and rape, once again, is in the news. One thing that these men and their infamous predecessors have in common is that their actions fit the stereotype of the 'perfect' rape: they and the victims are total strangers; their attacks are clearly premeditated and elaborately planned, often taking place in the victim's home after a break-in; they are often armed and usually inflict a good deal of physical injury in addition to the rape; and they generally commit a whole series of similar offences.

Paradoxically, though, the various institutions involved in the official processing of rape are at their best when dealing with offenders of precisely this type. Rape complaints in the area in question are taken seriously, as is the hunt for the perpetrator of the crimes. When he is caught and tried, he is very likely to plead guilty in the face of overwhelming evidence and is usually imprisoned for a very long time, not infrequently for life.

But for the majority of rapes, the story is not so straightforward, and in addition to the trauma of being raped, victims are more

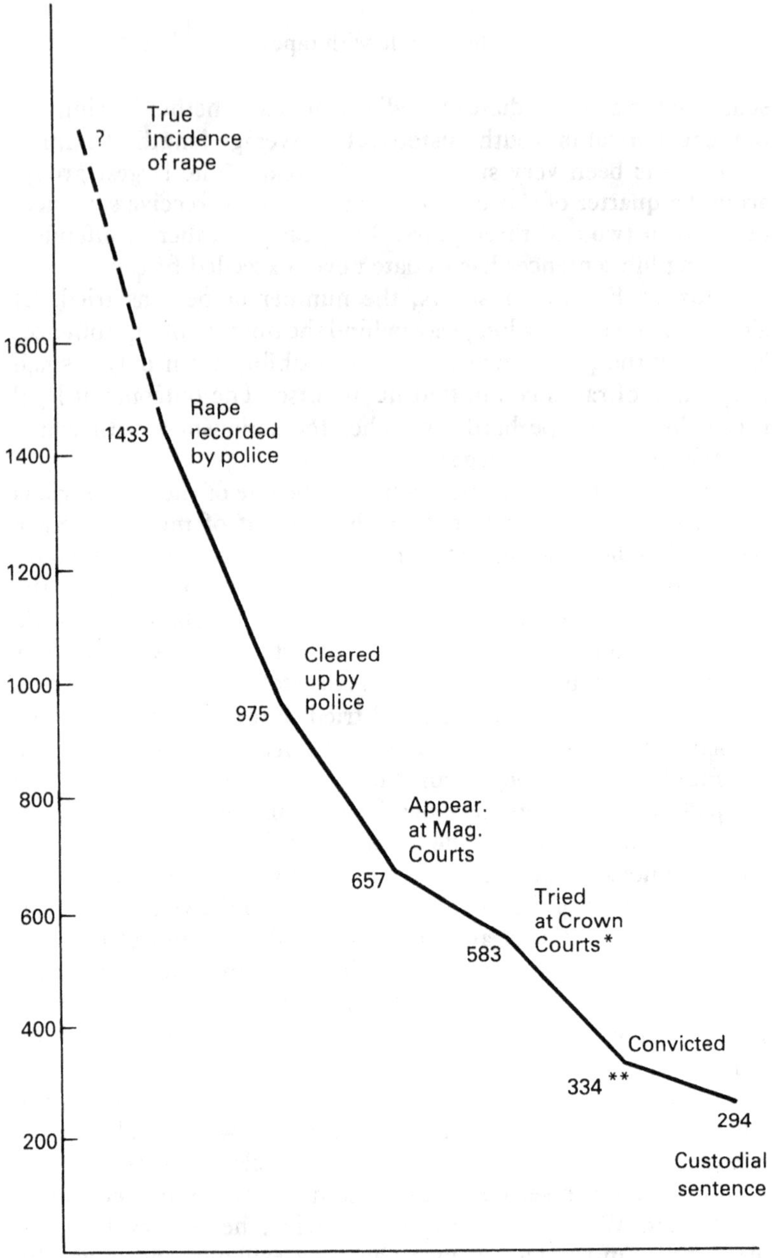

True incidence of rape
?
1600
1400
1200
1000
800
600
400
200
1433
Rape recorded by police
975
Cleared up by police
657
Appear. at Mag. Courts
583
Tried at Crown Courts*
334 **
Convicted
294
Custodial sentence

* There is some discontinuity here: although 583 persons were committed for trial at Crown Courts in 1984, only 454 had in fact been tried by the end of the year for which the statistics were compiled.

** Including those convicted at Magistrates' Courts.

Source: Criminal Statistics, 1984

Figure 1.1: *The disposition of reported rapes in 1984*

than likely to be exposed to a great deal of suspicious, harsh and often downright hostile treatment by the police and the courts. The roots of this lie in the traditional view of rape as an explosive expression of pent-up sexual impulse, the act of a man who, once aroused, is totally unable to control his sexual urges. One judge justified a six-month sentence on a teenage rapist by the classic remark that his sexual desires at his age were probably greater than in older people. Statements like 'he succumbed to the temptation' or 'he was unable to control himself' are often made in pleas in mitigation.

The view that a man rapes because he is sexually aroused leads the courts to assume that his victim must have stimulated him in some way, through her appearance, attitudes and behaviour. This notion tends to shift the attention and, ultimately, the responsibility, from the accused to the victim: at the trial, it is her conduct and actions that are most closely and harshly scrutinised. The range of unacceptable and provocative behaviours is extensive: she may be criticised for going to a pub or a dance by herself, for getting into a car with someone she didn't know well, for being out alone late at night, for letting an acquaintance into her house, for leaving her windows open, and indeed for sleeping in scanty nightclothes.

As we shall see below, the notion that men cannot help themselves is one of the most fundamental misconceptions about rape, but other equally powerful myths flourish, and continue to have a profoundly damaging effect on the way the police and the courts, as well as the press and the general public, view and deal with the offence of rape.

One of these is that when women refuse intercourse, they do not really mean it. Their protests are not to be taken seriously, as they probably just want to be seduced. The notion that women do not know their own minds and automatically indulge in dubious sexual games is not uncommonly underlined for the jury by well-meaning judges. Judge Wild at Cambridge Crown Court had this to say in 1982:

'Women who say no do not always mean no. It is not just a question of saying no, it is a question of how she says it, how she shows and makes it clear. If she doesn't want it she only has to keep her legs shut and she

9

would not get it without force and there would be marks of force being used.[17]

The impact of this myth on juries is powerful, and they can be persuaded that the woman's verbal refusal of intercourse does not signify lack of consent. In one Old Bailey trial, the defendant was acquitted by the jury after effectively admitting the offence in cross-examination:

Prosecution counsel: And you say she consented?
Defendant: I didn't say she consented, or that she didn't.
Prosecution council: Did she agree?
Defendant: She didn't agree.
Prosecution counsel: Having said no at first, she just gave in?
Defendant: She enjoyed it.
Judge: The enjoyment wiped out her initial resistance – is that what you are saying?
Defendant: Yes.

This is linked to another myth, namely that women enjoy being treated with force and violence. Indeed, it is said that many women fantasise about rape, so that when they claim that it has actually happened to them they may well have imagined it, or even invited it and enjoyed it.

An interesting aside is that Freud, together with his followers, lent a degree of pseudo-scientific respectability to the concept of female masochism.[18] While in all his works, he failed to consider the phenomenon of rape or to shed any light on the psychology of rapists, he did lay the foundations for subsequent studies on female fantasies of rape which he saw as a subconscious wish to be sexually overcome.

In his early writings Freud reported that a disproportionately high number of his female hysterical patients had, in their childhood, been 'seduced' by adults, particularly their fathers or older children. From the experience of his patients, he concluded that a passive sexual experience before puberty was the specific cause of hysteria in adult life. But some years later, he rejected his early theory. He wrote that he had made a mistake in accepting as true his patients' accounts of childhood seduction by their father, and he reinterpreted these as false memories which were in fact wishful fantasies, pointing to the existence of the Oedipus complex. However, there is nothing beyond conjecture to support his theories in this respect. Indeed, his basis for the contention that women fantasise about rape is his application of the layman's suspicion to his patients' accounts of sexual assault. He himself, rather more generously, attributed his initial 'mistake' to his lack of experience and admitted that at that time, he was unable to distinguish between his patients' fantasies about their childhood years and their true memories.

The notion that women fantasise about rape, and indeed are unable to distinguish between reality and fantasy in this respect, developed together with the idea that rape was something that women actually desired. Freud was the first to write in any depth of the nature of feminine masochism, which he saw as the ultimate in sexual maturity. These views were later expanded by post-Freudians who developed his basic theory of feminine masochism, the effects of which are still, sadly, very much reflected in contemporary attitudes towards women who have been raped.

Recent research findings strongly contradict the traditional view of rape as the result of sexual arousal, and establish that it is in fact an act of violence and aggression, reflecting the assailant's feelings of inferiority or inadequacy.[19] Far from being primarily motivated by the offender's sexual needs, rape is the sexual expression of frustration and anger. One convicted rapist reflects on his own motives in the following terms:

People talk about a sex drive. I don't think a sex drive drove me to do things. I think that I was feeling so rotten, so low and such a creep and I had so many secrets from everybody about myself that I got caught up in a lot of fantasy.[20]

There is now a considerable weight of evidence on this issue, based on careful clinical study of rape offenders. Nevertheless, the belief that rape is the outcome of frustrated sexual needs persists – and this belief provides the basis for a whole series of misconceptions about both victim and offender. So long as rape is seen as an act of sexuality rather than aggression and hostility, it will continue to be interpreted as predominantly pleasurable to both parties, rather than as harmful to the victim. Yet common sense, as well as ample evidence, show that rape is extremely damaging to the victim in a number of ways.

The first major empirical study of rape which was conducted in the early 1970s in the USA considered, among other things, the degree of violence involved in rape incidents, and found that some physical force had been used in 85 per cent of the cases studied.[21] The degree of force ranged from roughness to choking and brutal beating; over a fifth of the victims needed hospitalisation for the treatment of severe lacerations, fractures and the like. A number of more recent studies confirm these findings. Holmstrom and Burgess,[22] for example, report that two-thirds of a sample of 146 sexual assault victims had visible bruises resulting from being hit with a weapon or with the assailant's hand or fist during the assault. Gynaecological injury was present in nearly 40 per cent of that sample. In addition to sustaining such injuries, some victims become pregnant. According to their own accounts, 13 per cent of the women who contacted the London Rape Crisis Centre over a period of two years became pregnant as a result of the rape.[23]

For others, rape results in vaginal or venereal infections, although no precise figures are available as to the incidence of these.

But the victim's trauma is not only physical: the long-term emotional harm she suffers is immense. She is left with varying but persistent degrees of guilt, shame, fear, anger and frustration. Holmstrom and Burgess, whose work has been referred to above, interviewed ninety-two adult rape victims admitted to hospital over a one-year period in an American town. On the basis of their analysis, they were the first to identify a typical reaction which they called rape trauma syndrome. The syndrome includes a wide range of physical, emotional and behavioural reactions. Immediate emotional responses may be expressed and manifested by visible evidence of acute anxiety, emotional breakdown and disruption of normal patterns of behaviour. As one victim describes her first reaction,

'I think it's a state of shock you're in. All I can say is that after it happens you are so frightened, that ... I was threatened if I said anything, and I went back to an empty house and I spent about four or five days off work, shutting doors, locking doors after me, hiding in bed and you know there is no way I would have communicated with anybody, any of it.'[24]

Others at this stage appear calm and collected, showing little external evidence of distress, a reaction which may reflect shock and disbelief. Whichever form it takes, this initial phase is followed by a period of outward adjustment which may be deceptive insofar as it often contains a large measure of denial and suppression, and does not represent the final resolution of the crisis. After this, depression and anxiety may set in, and the long-term process of resolution begins. How long this takes varies from person to person, and depends on factors such as the victim's personality characteristics, the available support system, and the treatment she encounters from others. Some rapes are not resolved for many years, perhaps never, as one victim describes:

'I had nightmares on and off for about ten years. I'd cry for no reason and shake for no reason and sweat for no reason. I found all sorts of things gave me the shakes: the smell of tobacco, and beer, I found that I couldn't really walk into a pub or a bar because those were the smells that I associated with this man. I didn't like anybody walking behind me. Frightened of the dark, had to have a light on, if anybody walked into my room, even my mother when I went to stay at home, I was practically out of the window by the time I realised who it was. My parents and my family found it too delicate a subject to talk about, and I didn't have the strength to insist on talking about it, so there was this kind of silence behind which I hid, and they hoped I would heal. In retrospect, I think that was a mistake. And that if I had been able to talk about it, I would have got over it sooner. And it's taken me many years to be able to talk about it without breaking down.'[25]

Various external factors may contribute to the intensity and complexity of the 'normal' reaction that rape victims express. These include cases where the assailant is a relative or someone in a position of trust, or where the victim is particularly vulnerable by virtue of existing psychological or medical problems. Age-specific issues can also contribute to the trauma, as in the case of children or young girls without sexual experience, and indeed in very old victims. A woman who had been physically and sexually abused by her stepfather from the age of 12 over several years describes the particular difficulties in confiding in anyone about her situation:

'I felt I couldn't do anything. I knew what I had to do, but I felt that if I did, I would hurt my mother. So for a long time I didn't say anything. I'm not the only one who went through it, not the only stepchild, I know of two others. And for a long time, I felt really guilty about it. I thought if I had done something about him, he wouldn't have hurt anyone else. But even when I told my mother what was going on, she didn't believe me. She said nothing, she just didn't do anything or say anything. No reaction at all, none whatsoever. She didn't believe me until one day, I'm not sure how old I was, she saw him.'[26]

The rape reaction in such cases may be aggravated and include a significant increase in physical illness, alcohol and drug abuse, suicide attempts and severe depression. In 1984, the deaths of two young women were reported in the national press, both following a recent experience of rape. One turned to drink and drugs, and died of an accidental overdose; the other hanged herself.

When a victim reports the rape to the police, she sets in motion a complex and lengthy process involving the legal system. Most studies on the institutional response to rape victims have found that such response, far from helping the victim in her recovery, contributes to and magnifies the initial trauma precipitated by the sexual attack. An American study, tracing the victim's steps throughout the police, medical and court systems, argued that the woman becomes doubly victimised through her contact with these agencies: first, by the crime, and second, by the societal reactions she encounters.[27]

The height of institutional victimisation comes with the trial. A number of researchers have commented on the 'rape of the courts', where the victim not only has to relive her experience in the formal setting of a public court, but where her prior lifestyle and sexual conduct frequently become exposed to considerable scrutiny by the defence. Her consent or lack of it is then judged not so much on the circumstances of the rape itself, but on her past reputation. Her sexual character is considered a crucial element of the facts on which the court decides the defendant's innocence or guilt.

An American study of forty victims reports that every one of them found their court appearance stressful, and that most of them showed visible signs of stress during the court procedure. Many reported that their court experience was as upsetting as the rape itself.[28] Another ethnographic study of seventeen rape trials concluded that 'the extent of trauma suffered by the victim in her contact with the legal system is in large measure due to the attitudes and consequent treatment of the victim by the law enforcement and court personnel with whom she deals'.[29] Clearly, the post-rape adjustment of rape victims cannot be discussed without reference to the impact of the legal system in this respect.

While the above mentioned studies are American, the ordeal of rape victims in court has been acknowledged in the English context too. Coote and Gill[30] have argued that where the defence is one of consent, and where there is little or no independent evidence, the defence strategy will normally be to discredit the victim as this is seen as the most effective way of ensuring an acquittal. Cross-examination tends to take a particularly insidious, personal line. In effect, the woman is put on trial and has the difficult task of establishing her innocence beyond reasonable doubt in order to prove the man's guilt. The Report of the Advisory Group on the Law of Rape, which will be discussed below, made a similar point:

although in a criminal case, it is the accused who is on trial, there is a risk that a rape case may become in effect a trial of the alleged victim ... whatever the outcome, the very fact of having been involved is liable, at present, to have embarrassing or even damaging consequences for the woman.[31]

In this respect, and indeed in many others, the rape victim occupies a unique position in the legal system which treats her with unequalled suspicion. This is reflected, for example, in the corroboration rule which requires the judge in a sexual offence trial to warn the jury against the danger of convicting on the evidence of the complainant alone. Lord Justice Salmon justifies this practice as follows:

Human experience has shown that girls and women do sometimes tell an entirely false story which is very easy to fabricate but extremely difficult to refute. Such stories are fabricated for all sorts of reasons, which I need not now enumerate, and sometimes for no reason at all.[32]

It should be noted that the corroboration warning is given not only in rape cases, but in all cases of sexual offences, irrespective of the complainant's sex. However, a brief look at the relevant criminal statistics indicates that the vast majority of indictable sexual offences are committed by men against women and children. In 1984, for example, 98 per cent of the defendants tried at Crown

Courts in England and Wales for sexual offences were men; and 83 per cent of the accused were tried for offences which by definition can only be committed against women or children, both male and female.

Although the elimination of the corroboration rule, recognised as grossly offensive to women and discriminatory, has been a major feature of rape law reform in other jurisdictions, there is no sign of it being abolished here. The image of the neurotic female, particularly prone to lying and sexual hysteria, continues to pervade societal as well as legal attitudes towards the rape victim.

At the same time, and rather curiously, the traditional notion of the seriousness of rape is based on the assumption that rape is essentially different from normal sexual acts. Convicted rapists are often described in the press as 'beasts', 'sex monsters', 'savages', and 'evil beyond belief'. As Jackson aptly observed,

There is an element of double-think here: the belief in rape as something apart from everyday expressions of sexuality exists side by side with the notion that rape is impossible, that it does not happen at all, that the victim is a woman who has changed her mind afterwards. It is simultaneously thought of both as a heinous crime and as a normal sexual encounter mislabelled criminal.[33]

In recent years, this utterly inconsistent view of the offence has been challenged by a number of feminist writers, who have argued that in a society which encourages male aggression and simultaneously associates female sexuality with passivity and submission, the basic elements of rape are involved in all heterosexual relationships. Jackson, in particular, has attempted to understand rape in terms of conventional sexual behaviour. She conceptualised sexuality as the outcome of a learning process whereby the individual develops a capacity to interpret and enact 'sexual scripts', which are linked to cultural notions of masculinity and femininity. She argued that 'normal' sexual relationships are built around sexual inequalities insofar as the participants' roles have been predefined as subordinate and superordinate. Thus, the scripts which underlie normal sexual behaviour, derived from generally accepted cultural norms, also provide potential motives for rape. In this light, rape is merely an extreme manifestation of our culturally accepted male–female relationships, the exercise of power by the former over the latter being a crucial aspect of those relationships. This has been viewed as a significant factor in the persistence of rape as a social problem.

It is in the wake of such ideas that the plight of the rape victim became a focus of considerable interest. In the USA at least, the definition of rape as a social problem was a probable by-product of the feminist movement. As Berger has noted,

Since the law has traditionally defined this crime as an act committed by men against women, it is fitting that the 'rediscovery' of rape should coincide with the growth of the women's movement. Prominent feminists and leading feminist publications have authored or printed many of the relevant writings on the subject. Movement women and their sympathisers have organised conferences and speak-outs, primarily aimed at lending psychological support to victims of rape and enhancing feminine consciousness generally. Feminists have been instrumental in establishing and running rape crisis centres, extending to victims such varied aids as escort services, group counselling and referrals to physicians, psychiatrists and lawyers. Women have also played a key role in lobbying for reforms in the law of rape.[34]

A parallel, if not quite so momentous, development occurred in this country. The first Rape Crisis Centre, offering a counselling service for victims of sexual assault, was opened in London in 1976; today there are such Centres in most major cities. The last ten years have also witnessed a tremendous upsurge in public interest over the subject. Academic and popular literature reflect an increased concern with the plight of the victim, and a desire to protect her from what is seen as particularly unfair treatment by the legal system. Post-1974 literature reflects three main concerns: first, the needs of victims; second, the inadequacies of institutional response to them, and third, the modification of laws concerning rape.

From this background, a partial challenge to the traditional and unique role occupied by the rape victim in the legal process was beginning to emerge. It was becoming increasingly clear that rape victims were systematically subjected to institutionalised sexism, which began with their treatment by the police, continued through the legal system, much influenced by notions of victim precipitation, and ended with the acquittal of many de facto rapists. The implications of such a state of affairs for the likely rate of reporting to the police were also beginning to dawn. Anonymity for victims was beginning to be advocated, in an effort to encourage more women to come forward and report rape.

The history of rape law, changing attitudes towards the victim, and their implications for the legal reforms which took place in the mid-1970s, will be discussed in the next chapter.

Chapter 2

The legal origins

———————◆———————

As with much of our criminal law, the definition of rape evolved almost entirely on the basis of common law. The Sexual Offences Act 1956 provided, with an admirable economy of language verging on the laconic, that 'it is an offence for a man to rape a woman'. The first statutory definition, which adds little to the old common law definition, appears in Section 1(1) of the Sexual Offences (Amendment) Act 1976:

A man commits rape if
(a) he has unlawful sexual intercourse with a woman who at the time of the intercourse does not consent to it; and
(b) at that time he knows that she does not consent to the intercourse or he is reckless as to whether she consents to it.

This may seem to leave little doubt as to what constitutes the offence, but the legal definition is not without controversy. Adverse comment has been made about the narrow definition of rape as being confined to penetration of the vagina by the penis, excluding other forms of non-consensual sexual penetration. The latter amount to buggery in the case of anal penetration, or indecent assault which covers a huge range of acts ranging from bottom pinching to penetration with various objects or forced oral-genital contact. Until very recently, the maximum penalty for indecent assault against a female over the age of 13 was two years, while the corresponding penalty for a similar offence against a male was ten years. It was not until 1985 that the two maxima were brought in line, and offences against males and females are now both subject to a top penalty of ten years' imprisonment.[1]

But what is the background to current legal definitions and

attitudes to rape? Early English law reflects much confusion as to whether rape was a crime against a woman's body, or against a man's property. There was certainly from the earliest times a sexual element in the offence, and its very definition hinged on the victim's prior status: unless she was a virgin beforehand, her complaint of rape had no validity. But the offence also had a strong property aspect to it: rape in Anglo-Saxon law included abduction as well as forcible sex. As one textbook of legal history explains,

if it had wronged the woman, it had wronged her kinsmen also, and they would have felt themselves seriously wronged even if she had given her consent and had, as we should say, eloped.[2]

During this early period, the woman could save the offender from his sentence by marrying him, provided that the judge and the families involved agreed. Otherwise, the penalties imposed varied with the gravity of the offence, and with the relative social status of victim and offender.[3] In Anglo-Saxon law, the punishment for rape was death, and it became castration and blinding during the reign of William the Conqueror.[4] Major changes in the law of rape took place during the reign of Edward I. In 1275, the first Statute of Westminster fixed the punishment of the offender at two years' imprisonment to be followed by a fine. The legal concept of rape had by this time broadened to include, at least in principle, the rape of non virgins: offences committed against married women and virgins became equally punishable, and the custom of redemption by marriage was banned. Ten years later, the second Statute of Westminster brought back the death penalty for rape.[5]

The legislative changes embodied in the Statutes of Westminster have been interpreted in various ways. Some have argued that the first Statute did nothing to diminish the gravity of the offence despite the small penalty it imposed. For the first time in statute law, the rape of virgins and non virgins was equally punishable and the policy of Crown prosecution, again for all rapes, was an acknowledgment of rape as an issue of public safety and state concern. The small penalty that was law for ten years was seen in this light as a way of easing the effect of those major transitions.[6] Most historians, however, have argued that the first Statute reduced the status of the offence to a trespass, punishable only by a light penalty, and that the death penalty was brought back in the second Statute because it was felt that the lenient attitude of 1275 encouraged the commission of the crime.[7]

But it was during the seventeenth century that many of the principles governing contemporary rape law were set forward by Lord Hale. As the Advisory Group on the Law of Rape commented in 1975,

the traditional common law definition, derived from a seventeenth-century writer and still in use, is that rape consists in having unlawful sexual intercourse with a woman without her consent, by force, fear or fraud.[8]

Since Hale's time, various statutes with relevance for particular aspects of rape law have been enacted. The death penalty for rape was abolished in 1841, and a substantial amount of case law has built up around various aspects of the offence. However, the essential ingredients of the contemporary offence had been firmly established by the eighteenth century and Hale's influence in this context has been considerable. His writings have been referred to by virtually every writer who has discussed rape, and it has been noted that the 'misogynistic bias that has pervaded law and practice concerning ... rape'[9] is largely attributable to these. A number of matters testify to this point, in particular the question of marital exemption in rape, the relevance of the woman's character and behaviour at the time of the offence, and the corroboration warning in rape trials.

In contemporary law, a man cannot be convicted of the rape of his wife, although he may be guilty of the rape of his ex-wife provided the marriage has legally ended. Hale summarised the reasoning behind this principle as follows:

the husband cannot be guilty of a rape committed by himself upon his lawful wife, for by their mutual matrimonial consent and contract, the wife hath given up herself in this kind unto her husband, which she cannot retract.[10]

Hale's justification of the marital exemption rule undoubtedly implies a view of woman as man's property within the contract of marriage. This view has been challenged on numerous occasions. Commentators have found it 'archaic'[11] and 'patently absurd'.[12] In contemporary society, it has also led to a highly anomalous situation insofar as women who are cohabiting without marriage are protected by rape law, while wives are not. A man can be charged with raping his cohabiting partner – how easy it will be for her to prove her case before the jury is another matter. However, even if a married couple have been living apart for years without some form of legal separation, the husband cannot be charged with raping his wife. Yet, as we shall see in Chapter 10, the Criminal Law Revision Committee's Fifteenth Report on Sexual Offences, published in 1984, did not recommend major changes to the current position. The issue of marital rape also arose during the parliamentary debates of the Sexual Offences (Amendment) Bill in 1976, as well as more recently in 1983, but no change in the law was made with regard to rape within marriage – an indication that members of the House of Commons are on the whole still prepared to concur with an opinion which is now several hundred years out of date.

Perhaps the most controversial element in the legal treatment of rape before 1976 was the admissibility of evidence about the woman's sexual character. The defence could bring in evidence that she was 'a woman of notoriously bad character for want of chastity or common decency'[13] or a prostitute.[14] Any sexual behaviour with the defendant on previous occasions was admissible as evidence, as was any 'immoral' behaviour with other men.[15]

Whatever he said about the woman's sexual past, the defendant was safe from cross-examination as to his previous convictions or character. This rule dates from 1898: previously, the defendant was not able to give evidence, and most of the common law on the cross-examination of the victim was well established by that time. In the trial of any other criminal offence, a defendant attacking the character of a prosecution witness would run the risk of being cross-examined as to any previous convictions. However, this did not usually apply to attacks on the woman's sexual reputation at a rape trial. This effectively put rape in a wholly different category to any other criminal offence in that it gave the defence what has been termed 'licence for sexual mud-slinging'.[16] Furthermore, it created a distinction between the complainant and other prosecution witnesses, insofar as an attack on the character of those other witnesses would have 'let in' the character of the accused. The general purpose of introducing evidence as to the woman's bad reputation was succinctly summarised by Robin Corbett, MP in his introduction to the Sexual Offences (Amendment) Bill:

a woman could often be subjected to hurtful and irrelevant cross-examination about her previous sexual history, on the seeming assumption that because the woman had had, for example, an abortion, or an illegitimate baby, or was even held to be promiscuous, that somehow excused the rape or, worse, suggested that rape was not possible against such a woman.[17]

Another of Hale's statements provides the basis of the corroboration rule in modern English law. Although independent evidence to support the woman's story in a rape case is not essential in law, it is the established practice to warn the jury against the danger of convicting a man on her uncorroborated word. This is what Hale had to say about the matter: '[it] must be remembered that [rape] is an accusation easily to be made and hard to be proved, and harder to be defended by the party accused, though never so innocent.'[18] Although Hale was probably referring to an informal complaint, his dictum has been interpreted in more recent times as applying to formal complaints to the police. In this sense at least, the statement is grossly inaccurate: rape is not an easy charge to allege, and neither is it difficult to rebut. A considerable volume of recent research findings illustrate the enormous difficulties facing a woman in a rape case, as well as the greater likelihood of acquittal in these as compared to other criminal cases.[19] Nevertheless, the cautionary rule remains.

Another peculiar feature of the law of rape is the rule relating to 'recent complaint'. In the trial of a rape offence, the prosecution may produce evidence that a complaint was made by the victim on the first opportunity which reasonably offered itself after the offence. Although evidence of recent complaint does not amount to corroboration as it does not come from an independent source, it may be taken to indicate consistency in the behaviour of a woman.

This rule also seems to stem from the notion that there is some essential difference between the victims of rape and those of other criminal offences. The assumption is that rape is particularly liable to involve false accusations, and that women complaining of rape ought therefore to be put to a more stringent test than persons reporting other crimes. The genuineness of the complaint appears to be judged primarily with reference to the character and behaviour of the woman involved, rather than those of the man on trial. Again, to quote Hale, the woman may give evidence upon oath, and is in law a competent witness, but the credibility of her testimony, and how far forth she is to be believed, must be left to the jury, and is more or less credible according to the circumstances of fact, that concur in that testimony. For instance, if the witness be of good fame, if she presently discovered the offence and made pursuit after the offender, showed circumstances and signs of the injury ... if the place wherein the fact was done was remote from people, inhabitants or passengers, if the offender fled from it; these and the like are concurring evidences to give greater probability to her testimony when proved by others as well as herself. But on the other side, if she concealed the injury for any considerable time after she had the opportunity to complain, if the place where the fact was supposed to be committed were near to inhabitants or common recourse or passage of passengers, and she made no outcry when the fact was supposed to be done, when and where it is probable she might be heard by others; these and the like circumstances carry a strong presumption that her testimony is false or feigned.[20]

The fear of false accusations is also reflected in the guidelines given to doctors regarding the medical examination of women reporting rape. One of the main sources of corroboration in modern rape trials is medical and forensic evidence regarding the identity of the parties involved, the occurrence of sexual intercourse and, most frequently, the physical injuries sustained by the woman as a result of the assault. Physical resistance to the attacker is frequently seen as an essential element of 'genuine' rape, while the absence of bodily injury to substantiate such resistance in a woman alleging rape is thought to be a good indication that the complaint is a false one.[21] One distinguished writer in the field of forensic medicine warns that 'a girl out of her first decade is seldom capable of being raped against her will [sic] without mark of forcible restraint or injury.'[22]

Although textbooks of legal medicine tend to give some acknowledgment to the possibility of submission through intimidation and fear, their main concern is with the interpretation of signs of injury and with the extent to which injuries are consistent with the woman's account of what happened. A questionable assumption is sometimes made that one must expect a greater degree of resistance in women accustomed to intercourse than in virgins, who are thought to be more likely to be 'terrified into inactivity'.[23]

The finding of physical injury alone, however, does not necessarily substantiate a woman's story and the doctor is warned that alternative explanations for any injury must always be looked for. For example, warns one textbook of forensic medicine, the doctor must consider the possibility that the victim may have 'lacerated the parts and stained the clothes with blood to simulate the condition'.[24]

Just what is the evidence on the incidence of false allegations of rape? A Scottish study of police response to rape published in 1984[25] showed that although some officers were given to a certain amount of rhetoric on this subject, they found it very difficult indeed to recall particular cases they had dealt with that were unquestionably false allegations. Yet such claims continue to be made with monotonous regularity: an experienced police woman was recently quoted as saying that, in her opinion, as many as nine out of ten allegations were unfounded.[26] Against this assertion, a senior police officer and the author of a book on the investigation of rape offences, argues that 'There can be no credible basis for the suggestion that 70 per cent, 50 per cent or even 20 per cent of allegations of sexual assaults are false, in the sense of being untrue.'[27]

Research in this area is rather thin on the ground, and its results conflicting. The Howard League's 1985 Report on Sexual Offences[28] quotes two British studies on this subject. One concludes that nearly 90 per cent of allegations are false,[29] and the other, that the figure is somewhere between 29 and 47 per cent.[30] Both were carried out by police surgeons on very small samples, without a comparison group and using questionable criteria for deciding the truth or otherwise of a complaint. The question of which criteria are used to decide truth or falsehood is crucial, and has not been addressed by either of these studies, or any others in this country to date. The only methodologically sound study originates from the USA, where the New York Sex Crimes Analysis Unit[31] looked systematically at all allegations made to them over a period of two years. They found that the rate of false allegations for rape and sexual offences was around 2 per cent, which was comparable to the rate for unfounded complaints of other criminal offences.

The basic assumption that women have a tendency to lie and make false and malicious accusations of rape has been a dominant theme in legal thinking from the earliest times to the present. That attitude, and the correspondingly deep suspicion towards women alleging rape, is reflected in the law of rape which sets the offence in a unique category within the general body of the criminal law in several fundamental respects. The Sexual Offences (Amendment) Act 1976 was generally seen as a move forward and away from old assumptions, as well as a genuine attempt at restoring some balance between the rights of the complainant and defendant in a rape trial. It came about as a result of widespread concern with the treatment of rape victims by the legal system, and was based on the recommendations of the Advisory Group on the Law of Rape, appointed following the controversial House of Lords ruling in the case of Morgan and others.

In that case, Morgan, an RAF pilot, invited three of his colleagues to go home with him after an evening spent drinking and have intercourse with his wife. He told them that although she may protest and struggle, they should not pay any attention because this turned her on. At the trial, the three younger men claimed that Mrs Morgan consented, and if she did not, they certainly thought that she did, on the basis of what her husband had told them earlier that evening. The judge directed the jury that the defendants should be acquitted if they honestly believed that the woman consented and if such belief was held on reasonable grounds. The men were convicted and subsequently appealed on the grounds that the trial judge misdirected the jury and that they were entitled to an acquittal if the jury found that the victim did not consent, provided they, the defendants, honestly believed that she did, whether the grounds for their belief were reasonable or not. The Court of Appeal (Criminal Division) dismissed the appeals which then went to the House of Lords.

Although the convictions of the men in the Morgan case were upheld, the majority of the Law Lords who considered the question held that a man should be acquitted of rape if he honestly believed that the woman consented, even if he did not have reasonable grounds for his belief. The rationale for that decision was that the ruling merely extended to the crime of rape a well-established principle of criminal law, namely that there should be in any criminal offence some blameworthy condition of the mind. This is seen as some sort of mental link between the accused person and the unlawful act he is alleged to have committed, but it is without doubt a difficult concept. The main point of disagreement among the Law Lords in the case of Morgan and others had, at its root, divergent interpretations as to what constituted established practice in various areas of the criminal law with regard to criteria used to determine the presence of a guilty mind.

Much literature has been devoted in this context to the cases of Smith and Hyam.[32] The decisions in these cases turn on whether the prosecution must establish that the defendant himself had the intent to commit the particular crime, or whether it would be enough to prove that an average person in a similar position would have had that intent. In the case of Smith, the House of Lords applied the objective test as to what a reasonable man would have foreseen and intended, and the appellant's conviction was upheld.

Section 8 of the Criminal Justice Act 1967, on the other hand, provides that a jury is not bound by law to infer that the particular defendant intended a result of his actions simply because that result was a natural and probable consequence of them. This has been interpreted as a subjective test, and was applied in the case of Hyam where the appellant's conviction was quashed.[33] A similar line of reasoning was followed in the case of Morgan and others by the majority of the Law Lords. This was Lord Hailsham's argument:

Once one has accepted, what seems to me abundantly clear, that the prohibited act in rape is non-consensual sexual intercourse, and that the guilty state of mind is an intention to commit it, it seems to me to follow as a matter of inexorable logic that there is no room either for a 'defence' of honest belief or mistake, or of a defence of honest and reasonable belief and mistake. Either the prosecution proves that the accused had the requisite intent, or it does not. ... I am content to rest my view of the instant case on the crime of rape by saying that it is my opinion that the prohibited act is and always has been intercourse without consent of the victim and the mental element is and always has been the intention to commit that act, or the equivalent intention of having intercourse willy nilly, not caring whether the victim consents or no. A failure to prove this involves an acquittal because the intent, an essential ingredient, is lacking. It matters not why it is lacking if only it is not there, and in particular it matters not that the intention is lacking only because of a belief not based on reasonable grounds.[34]

The dissenters, Lord Simon of Glaisdale and Lord Edmund Davies, referred to a number of cases where judgments seemed to indicate that in some circumstances at least, the objective test was held to be the correct one. Indeed, they pointed out that recent statute law in the area of sexual offences confirmed this view. According to s. 6(3) of the Sexual Offences Act 1956, a man is not guilty of unlawful sexual intercourse with a girl under the age of 16 if he is under the age of 24, has not previously been charged with a similar offence, believes her to be of the age of 16 or over and has reasonable cause for the belief. Hence, it was argued, the

necessary course is to uphold, as being in accordance with established law, the direction given in this case by the learned trial judge as to the necessity for the mistake of fact urged to be based on reasonable grounds.[35]

Lord Simon of Glaisdale also took into account the position of the victim in coming to his decision. He interpreted what in his opinion was established policy as derived from legal concern to strike a fair balance between the victim and the accused:

A respectable woman who has been ravished would hardly feel that she was vindicated by being told that her assailant must go unpunished because he believed, quite unreasonably, that she was consenting to sexual intercourse with him.[36]

While respectability has little to do with this argument, Lord Simon certainly has a valid point about the potential effect of the judgment on the feelings of all rape victims. In any event, the Lords' majority decision provoked considerable public controversy. Legal opinion was generally in favour of it and confirmed it as nothing more than the welcome application of accepted principles of criminal law to the offence of rape. The National Council for Civil Liberties also supported the decision and an article in *New Society* commented that, as a matter of logic, the ruling was quite right.[37]

However, the mere fact that the Court of Appeal dismissed the appeals yet gave leave to appeal to the House of Lords indicates a feeling that the issues involved here were far from simple. A reading of the House of Lords' judgments reveals that the main issues in the case were open to a good deal of interpretation. In particular, there was disagreement regarding the definition of the general principles of the law relating to criminal liability as well as the application to such principles to the offence of rape. The Law Lords' inability to reach a unanimous decision on the matter also underlines the fact that there was at least some degree of doubt, at that stage, as to the correctness of the majority view.[38]

Popular opinion and the media in general were fiercely opposed to the Morgan ruling. The *Sunday Mirror* labelled it a 'Rapists' Charter',[39] and this feeling was reflected in numerous articles and readers' letters in most daily newspapers. These expressed the fear of 'bogus defences' and of men 'getting away' with rape, which was felt to be the inevitable consequence of the ruling:

> The scales of justice have swung heavily in favour of rapists. . . . Henceforth, every rapist will declare his 'belief' that his victim was willing – and expect his ticket to freedom . . . because the principle that a man's belief, if he can convince the jury of it, can prevent conviction is now enshrined unassailably in law.[40]

A reconsideration of the law was urgently called for by a number of individuals and organisations. The National Council of Women of Great Britain, for example, asked for Parliament to 'take immediate steps to reform the intolerable state of this section of the criminal law'.[41]

One immediate response to the Lords' ruling was the presentation in Parliament of a Bill containing three major proposals for the reform of rape law.[42] It was introduced by Jack Ashley MP. The first proposal was aimed at reversing the Law Lords' ruling in the Morgan case, and at replacing the subjective test adopted in the ruling by an objective test. The second proposal was to grant anonymity for victims of rape, except by direction of the court. Thirdly, the Bill sought to ban the disclosure in court of the woman's sexual experience prior to the rape as this was felt to be irrelevant to her credibility or her consent.

Although the Home Secretary initially declined to take emergency action to reverse the Lords' ruling, he eventually agreed, in the face of mounting public pressure, to consider the matter further. He announced that he would be seeking the advice of an independent group which would consider the controversial judgment in a wider context. The Advisory Group on the Law of Rape was appointed in July 1975, under the chairmanship of Mrs Justice Heilbron, with the following terms of reference: 'To give consideration to the law of rape in the light of recent public concern and to advise the Home Secretary whether early changes in the law are desirable.'[43] In appointing the Group, the Home Secretary appeared to have given in to public pressure and agitation resulting directly from the Law Lords' decision in the case of Morgan. However, it has been noted that the setting up of the group was a 'very curious intervention',[44] and that the Morgan decision ought not to have been considered in relation to the offence of rape alone. It has also been argued that such an ad hoc approach was inappropriate to law reform, particularly when sexual offences in general were already being considered by the Criminal Law Revision Committee. Rape was felt to be 'especially unsuited to instant responses to popular commotions'.[45]

A number of other factors inherent in the social climate probably favoured a reappraisal of the law of rape at that stage. It has been argued that a distinction can be made between attitudes towards violent crime on the political and personal level, relating to concern over rising crime rates and to personal fear of crime respectively. As far as the 'political level' in England was concerned, the events leading to law reform in 1975 took place against a background of unprecedented increase in the reported number of rapes. The yearly number known to the police more than doubled between 1960 and 1978, and, for the first time, exceeded the thousand mark in 1974.

The importance of fear as a factor governing public opinion about rape has been pointed out by Sutherland in the North American context.[46] He identified a typical course of events leading to the enactment of what have been termed sexual psychopath laws in the USA. The first essential ingredient of legislative reform, he argued, was a state of fear aroused in the community when a few serious sexual crimes have been committed in rapid succession. This is usually accompanied by nationwide publicity and considerable agitation in the community. Whatever the general level of fear of rape in the community at any particular point in time, this was substantially increased as a result of the activities between September 1974 and May 1975 of the man who became known as the Cambridge rapist. The case received nationwide press publicity and public concern increased as it appeared that the rapes were becoming more violent on each occasion. Some of the victims suffered considerable injuries requiring hospitalisation and even surgical intervention. The local community was in a state of panic: 'Talk of the rapes is everywhere. . . . Rumours fly about wildly. . . . False alarms continue.'[47]

By May 1975, the panic and the hunt for the Cambridge rapist had reached such proportions that reports of the latest attack, an unsuccessful attempt, and police efforts to catch the man vied for space in the national press with news of the Lords' judgment in the case of Morgan.

The popular view of rape as an extremely serious crime was underlined by the Cambridge events, and the Law Lords' judgment in that light was interpreted as a denial of the gravity of the offence. It was widely believed that the ease of putting up a bogus defence would have the effect of deterring rape complaints and that increasing numbers of rapists would go undetected and unpunished. A concern with encouraging women to report rape was one of the key issues in the proposals for providing anonymity to victims of rape; this was initially brought up in the House of Commons in 1974, before Jack Ashley's Bill.

Chibnall[48] has argued that in reporting violence, the press tend to emphasise whatever sexual connotation is available. Thus, rape victims are usually described in the press in terms of their marital status, age, physical appearance and other personal attributes. It has also been noted that some papers, particularly after an acquittal, tend to include somewhat gratuitous remarks about the private life of the victim. Examples quoted by Soothill and Jack, on the basis of an extensive review of newspaper reporting of rape, include statements such as 'Mrs D. said she had been living with a coloured man for nine months', and 'Mrs S. answered the door wearing only baby doll pyjamas and invited him in for a cup of tea'.[49] More recently, and much more viciously, a headline in *The Times* described the victim of a multiple indecent assault as a 'sex maniac'.[50]

Thus, the ordeal for women of giving evidence at the trial and of being cross-examined on intimate details of their personal lives was in many cases compounded by full-scale publicity. A number of questions were asked in the House of Commons in 1974 regarding the possible provision of anonymity for women at rape trials, but these questions only received the answer that judges already had sufficient discretion in this matter without further legislation. However, existing practice was regarded as inconsistent by many, and criticised for being dependent on 'the judge's view of the deserving character of the woman'.[51]

The Rape (Anonymity of Victims) Bill was introduced by F. P. Crowder MP in July 1974. This Bill was intended to encourage victims to come forward and make statements to the police without fear of publicity, and was described by its sponsor as an un-controversial measure. It was concerned with the need to protect the 'genuine' victim, but because of the perceived danger of en-couraging false accusations, it did not intend to provide full-scale anonymity on all occasions. It would have kept the victim's name unpublished during the proceedings, but would then have vested the judge with authority to direct, on application by the defence, that her name be revealed in cases where she 'out of spite and venom ... quite unjustly and wrongfully'[52] made a false accusation.

Although Crowder's Bill did not go beyond a first reading, the question of anonymity remained a live issue throughout 1974 and 1975. The Bill was reintroduced in early 1975, and its main provisions were also incorporated in Ashley's Bill in June 1975. The matter was also considered by the Heilbron Group, and the Sexual Offences (Amendment) Act 1976 includes an anonymity provision for women in rape cases.

As the Home Secretary intended, the Advisory Group on the Law of Rape under the chairmanship of Mrs Justice Heilbron considered a number of issues relevant to the law of rape in addition to the Lords' decision in Morgan, and its recommendations covered the definition of the offence, the question of evidence, the anonymity of women and the composition of juries. Written and oral evidence was sought from a variety of individuals and organ-isations from the legal and medical professions, the police, women's groups and the media. Information was also received from other countries and the Group studied the Bills which had been pre-sented in Parliament by Ashley and Crowder respectively. The evidence presented to the Heilbron Group reflected the controversy that had characterised public response to the Morgan ruling, although interestingly, that issue was perhaps least disputed among the matters considered by the Group.

The Group's report was published in December 1975. Although most of its recommendations concerned the conduct of rape trials, the need for a statutory definition of rape was stressed from the outset. It was felt that a comprehensive definition emphasising lack of consent rather than violence as the essential ingredient of the offence was required, as the absence of a statutory definition had in the past caused some difficulty. Furthermore, the Group argued that although the decision in Morgan was right in principle, it would be desirable to clarify the point by incorporating in a statutory definition some reference to the law governing intention in rape cases.

Much of the evidence received by the Group criticised the practice and procedure followed in rape trials rather than the substantive law of rape or indeed the decision in the case of Morgan. The Group acknowledged the prolonged ordeal, humiliation and distress that the woman was likely to suffer during cross-examination. While emphasising that every accused person must have a fair trial, the Group argued that some restriction ought to be placed on the kind of cross-examination which effectively put the woman herself on trial, without advancing the cause of justice. In considering this, the Group outlined their approach as follows:

We have reached the conclusion that the previous sexual history of the alleged victim with third parties is of no significance so far as credibility is concerned, and is only rarely likely to be relevant to issues directly before the jury. In contemporary society, sexual relationships outside marriage, both steady and of a more casual character, are fairly widespread, and it seems now to be agreed that a woman's sexual experiences with partners of her own choice are neither indicative of untruthfulness nor of a general willingness to consent. There exists, in our view, a gap between the assumptions underlying the law and those public views and attitudes which exist today which ought to influence today's law.[53]

It was felt that the relationship of the woman and the accused would generally be relevant to the issues in the trial and should remain admissible in evidence. However, the Group strongly argued that her sexual history with anyone else, including the general question of 'bad reputation', ought not to be admissible, subject to one important exception. The trial judge would have the discretion to admit such evidence, according to principles set out in legislation as follows:

if the judge is satisfied –
(a) that this evidence relates to behaviour on the part of the complainant which was strikingly similar to her alleged behaviour on the occasion

of, or in relation to, events immediately preceding or following the alleged offence; and

(b) that the degree of relevance of that evidence to issues arising in the trial is such that it would be unfair to the accused to exclude it.[54]

The Group also acknowledged that women in rape cases can be greatly distressed by the publicity to which they may be exposed, and that there was widespread support for providing anonymity for women in such cases. They rejected the idea of holding rape trials in camera, and argued that any exception to the full reporting of criminal proceedings should be especially justified. They concluded that women in rape cases should, in general, be given protection from identification in the media.

They rejected the view incorporated in the earlier Crowder Bill that the judge should have discretion to release the woman's name where, in his opinion, she had lied or brought a false charge. The publication of the woman's name in such circumstances would be a penal measure, and punishment without a trial would be wrong in principle. Also, it was again stressed that the rape trial ought not to be treated as the trial of the woman. It was recommended that the anonymity restriction should only be lifted where her identity was necessary for the discovery of potential witnesses at the trial.

The final set of recommendations concerned the composition of juries. The Group's opinion was that both sexes should be adequately represented and recommended that there should be a minimum of four women and also four men on all rape juries.

Some of the Group's recommendations were received with reservations. In particular, the Report was criticised for going too far in protecting women against publicity. *The Times* argued that women making malicious and entirely untruthful allegations should not 'escape unscathed, either by the law or by publicity', and suggested that the trial judge have the discretion to reveal the woman's name in cases where her behaviour 'amounts to or approaches gross perjury'.[55]

Nevertheless, the Report was on the whole well received. Its recommendations were seen as a major step forward in protecting rape victims, and in persuading them to report the offence to the police. It was called a 'sensible and sensitive report'[56] and although it contained no proposal to reverse the Morgan ruling, some of the popular press even dubbed it a 'Charter for rape victims'.[57]

The Heilbron Report constitutes the basis of the Sexual Offences (Amendment) Bill, which was drafted by parliamentary draftsmen and had full government support although it was introduced as a Private Member's Bill. Initially, it incorporated all of the Advisory Group's recommendations, with the exception of the one concerning the composition of juries. This was rejected as it was felt that interference with the random selection of juries may extend to the trial of other offences, and that such a fundamental change in an important aspect of the legal system was not justified.

At the Committee stage, a new clause was introduced regarding anonymity for defendants in rape cases. Because of the potential consequences of a groundless accusation for an innocent man, it was argued that the defendant too should be covered by an anonymity provision, to be lifted in the event of a conviction. A number of Members opposed this clause, because the principle of singling out defendants in rape trials for special treatment was felt to go against the core of the criminal justice system. However, the proposition to grant anonymity to defendants gained support from the majority of the House, particularly from those who saw outright anonymity for women as a dangerous measure which would encourage malicious accusations. Taking his lead from Hale, one QC warned that

there is no branch of law, no class of case, where it is so easy for a woman to make an allegation of this kind and to make it against a professional man. It is men too who require protection of their reputations against baseless allegations of rape, which frequently occur.[58]

The clause regarding anonymity for defendants, which was incorporated in the Act, was thus seen as an attempt at redressing the balance between woman and accused, and at ensuring that false accusations would not be made too lightly from 'acute jealousy or from morbid feelings of having been rejected' by 'emotionally and psychologically unbalanced' women.[59]

Debates on matters of crime and penal policy in the Commons tend to have considerable input from members of the legal profession, and the debates of the Sexual Offences (Amendment) Bill were no exception. They were dominated throughout by lawyers from both sides of the House, claiming expertise in this field by virtue of their experience in criminal trials in general and rape trials in particular. Indeed, the tone of the debate occasionally suggested open conflict between lawyers and non-lawyers: the Heilbron Group, not predominantly composed of members of the legal profession, was said to have 'transgressed into the criminal law with insufficient experience of what it was seeking to do'.[60] This criticism was made particularly strongly in connection with recommendations to limit the scope of cross-examination, where it was felt that the proposed legislation represented an intrusion into the professional autonomy of lawyers.

Individual opinions were legitimated by reference to professional expertise: while the Heilbron Group felt that a woman's sexual experience was generally irrelevant to her consent or credibility when she made an allegation of rape, there was considerable support in the House for the view that this was at least likely to be relevant to the question of consent. Frequent reference was made in this context to cases where the woman was of 'thoroughly ill repute in sexual matters',[61] and one Member observed that 'a woman with a past ... is less likely to be the victim of rape than a maiden aunt, an unpromiscuous virgin, or a respectable married woman'.[62]

The relevant clause was eventually redrafted, partly as a concession to the views outlined above, and partly as a result of influential objections voiced in the House of Lords about the complexity of the proposed legislation. It was simplified, and did not lay down any rules for judges to follow in considering applications to admit evidence of this kind, beyond the matter of unfairness to the defendant. In principle, the Act conceded that a woman's previous sexual experience should not be a matter for the court to consider in trying to decide whether or not she has been raped. In practice, however, it left the decision as to whether this sort of evidence is relevant in any particular case entirely up to the trial judge.

The Sexual Offences (Amendment) Act 1976 became law on 22 November 1976. Its sponsors described it as a victory for the rape victim, and as a measure which would encourage women to come forward and report sexual assaults:

It will not make it easy for a woman who has suffered this appalling ordeal to report it. What I hope it will do is to make it less difficult to report and, without taking away any right from the defendant, give added protection to the growing numbers of women to whom this vilest of crimes will become a terrifying reality.[63]

However, the Act was not quite the unmitigated success that the above statement suggests. For every concession made to the victim, there was some counter-measure which favoured the defendant. In the first instance, the Act reinforced the Law Lords' decision in the case of Morgan which had caused such furore. Secondly, although it granted anonymity to complainants in rape cases, it also extended this to defendants. Interestingly, victims of blackmail are also protected by anonymity but the provision in those cases does not extend to the accused; the logic of granting anonymity to both parties in rape cases is, to say the least, unusual. Finally, the Heilbron Group recommended that evidence of the woman's previous sexual experience should only be admitted in exceptional cases, and that the trial judge be guided by principles set out in legislation in considering whether or not to admit such evidence. However, in the final event, one is left with a piece of legislation which leaves the grounds for the admissibility of such evidence entirely to the discretion of the trial judge.[64] No guiding principles are laid down in legislation beyond the vague and unsatisfactory criterion of fairness to the defendant. Evidence becomes relevant if the judge deems it to be so, which is an absurd state of affairs if the law is intended to be applied in a consistent and uniform manner.

One of the major objectives of the Sexual Offences (Amendment) Act 1976 was to rectify the earlier position where the victim of rape was in effect as much on trial as the defendant. The Act has been described as a 'response to feminist agitation about the absence of adequate concern for rape victims in Britain'.[65] Somewhat more cynically, however, it can be seen as a mere concession to popular agitation rather than a meaningful change in legal attitudes towards rape victims. Any discussion of the significance and impact of this piece of legislation must be based on its application in the courts. In what circumstances do judges allow the woman's name to be published? How frequently are applications made by the defence to cross-examine the woman on her previous sexual experience? What grounds are put forward to justify the need for such cross-examination? How do judges rule on these applications? What types of criteria emerge in determining the relevance of various matters under application? Does evidence of this sort continue to be introduced without an application to the judge, and if so, in what circumstances? How far is the law adhered to? Is the outcome of the trial likely to be affected by the introduction of evidence of sexual character? To what extent, if at all, does the Court of Appeal intervene in the exercise of discretion of trial judges?

The study on which this book is based was designed to answer some of the above questions, on the basis of material collected from trials for rape offences conducted at the Central Criminal Court.

Chapter 3

Rape cases at the Old Bailey

The majority of prosecutions for rape offences committed in the Greater London area take place at the Central Criminal Court, also known as the Old Bailey. Not uncommonly, several rape cases are running concurrently in the numerous courts of this large building and its annexe. Contested cases can last anything from two days to several weeks, with an average of about five working days. A random 85 per cent of the rape trials heard at the courts during a one-year period were included in this study. The material obtained provides a representative picture of the legal handling of rape cases in London, but the findings are also of relevance to the trial of offences elsewhere in the country: a substantial proportion of Old Bailey cases are tried by High Court judges who travel from one Crown Court to another, and whose impact on the case is unlikely to vary with geographical location.

Detailed field notes were taken, as verbatim as possible, of the circumstances of the case, the evidence, legal submissions, judicial directions, verdict and sentencing in the eighty-one trials included in this study. All quotations from evidence, cross-examination and speeches used in this book are based on these notes, and accurately represent what was said in court. In addition, all convictions were followed up in the Court of Appeal (Criminal Division), and records of appeals against conviction and/or sentence examined. This served a number of purposes. First, decisions in the Court of Appeal can drastically alter the outcome of trials: sentences may be varied, and convictions quashed. Such decisions must clearly be considered if one is to have a complete picture of the criminal process as it relates to rape. Second, in considering the application of the 1976 Act, it is essential to examine whether and how far the Court of Appeal is willing to interfere with the discretion of trial

39

judges with respect to the admission of sexual history evidence. Third, examination of Court of Appeal files provided a useful reliability check for parts of the data collected during the trials themselves: field notes of cases were checked against the transcripts contained in the files of the Court of Appeal.

Empirical research based on observation of court procedure is in fact the only reliable and valid way of obtaining answers to some of the questions that have arisen in recent years about the treatment of rape and its victims by the courts. Official statistics provide a limited amount of factual information about the number of defendants tried each year, the outcome of trials, sentencing, and so on, but they do not convey anything of the nature and quality of decision-making in court. Newspaper reporting is too superficial, patchy and often inaccurate to be useful as the basis of any systematic study. The other possible source material might be the shorthand note which is taken of all the evidence, and of the judge's summing up at every trial. However, this remains in shorthand form unless particular aspects of it are needed for an appeal, and even then only extracts relevant to the substance of the appeal are transcribed. Thus, transcripts of applications to introduce evidence of the woman's sexual experience would be available only when the trial judge had refused permission to cross-examine, and this decision had become the grounds of an appeal following conviction. This occurred only once in the trials included in this study.

The Old Bailey and its judges

The Central Criminal Court was established in 1834 for the trial of offences committed in London, Middlesex and some parts of Essex, Hertford, Kent and Surrey. It became a Crown Court in 1971, but still retains much of the tradition and ceremonial associated with its former role as the court of the City of London. Two types of judges sitting at the Court have jurisdiction to try rape cases: visiting High Court judges, and permanent circuit judges, including the Recorder of London, who is the judge of the Central Criminal Court, and the Common Serjeant. Just under half of the cases in this study were tried by circuit judges, while the Recorder of London alone presided over an impressive 18 per cent. The remainder went to the visiting High Court judges. As mentioned in Chapter 1, the Lord Chancellor directed that only senior judges authorised to try murders should preside over rape cases since the completion of this research. This new direction would have affected about a quarter of rape cases tried at the Central Criminal Court had it been implemented before the data collection period.

It is a well-known fact that the legal profession, particularly at the higher echelons, is dominated by men. Out of a total of 339 circuit judges, only ten are women. The first woman High Court judge was appointed in 1965, and women currently number three out of seventy-seven High Court judges. No woman has ever sat on the Judicial Committee of the House of Lords.

Judges trying rape cases at the Old Bailey were, without exception, men. A recent publication by the National Council on Civil Liberties comments on the narrow recruitment base of British judges:

A typical profile of all those High Court judges appointed between 1980 and 1982 is of a 55-year-old white male, educated at one of the top public schools and Oxbridge, and an experienced barrister and QC.[1]

The Old Bailey rape judges certainly conform to this average in terms of educational and professional background. However, whether they were circuit or High Court judges, their average age at the time of these trials was 65.

The overwhelming majority (90 per cent) of barristers appearing on either side in rape cases are men, and this reflects the overall sex composition of the profession. Interestingly, however, such women as do appear in rape trials tend to prosecute rather than defend. Women are a little better represented among instructing solicitors on both sides, but are still very much in a minority. Police officers in charge of the cases, usually of Detective Inspector rank, are again almost invariably men. It is quite possible to walk into a court and only see one woman, the shorthand-writer. Once the jury is brought in, the sex ratio improves a little, although the better representation of women on juries is a relatively recent phenomenon. Nevertheless, only half of the rape juries consisted of equal numbers of men and women; for the remainder, women were much more likely to be under, rather than overrepresented.

This overwhelming male presence in court is not, of course, confined to rape cases, but its implications for the victims of a crime which by definition is committed by men against women are considerable, and will be discussed in greater detail below.

The trials

The eighty-one trials in this study involved a total of 112 men accused of rape offences against 102 girls and women. The majority (81 per cent) were charged with the full offence of rape, and the rest, with an attempt or aiding and abetting rape. The offences were fairly evenly distributed throughout the Greater London area, although some police stations, particularly in the more deprived parts of the city, had more than their share of rape cases to handle.

Less than half of the men in this study were charged with rape offences alone. Twenty-nine per cent were also accused of additional sexual offences, such as, for example, unlawful sexual intercourse (i.e. intercourse with a girl under the age of consent), incest or buggery against the same victim. A similar proportion were charged with offences against the person, such as assault occasioning actual or grievous bodily harm. The substance of these offences is usually the violence deployed, before, during or after, but always in addition to the rape. Where there is evidence indicating the use of considerable physical force, such as severe beatings, gagging, attempts at strangling, and so on, the defendant is often charged with some sort of assault. However, more minor injuries inflicted in the course of rape, such as bruising and superficial scratching, do not normally form the basis of a separate charge. Another 20 per cent of the accused were charged with property offences, such as criminal damage, arising, for example, from kicking a door down in the course of entering the victim's premises, or theft, when in addition to rape, the defendant was also alleged to have made off with the woman's money, jewellery, or any other property.

Twenty-nine per cent of the men included in the study pleaded 'guilty' to rape, or some lesser offence that was acceptable to the Crown. The rest contested the charge and had a full trial. Figure 3.1 shows the precise breakdown of pleas, charges and outcome of trials for all defendants – the latter, together with sentencing, will be discussed in Chapter 8.

In the majority of cases, a single defendant was charged in any one trial, but a substantial number of trials involved more than

Rape cases at the Old Bailey

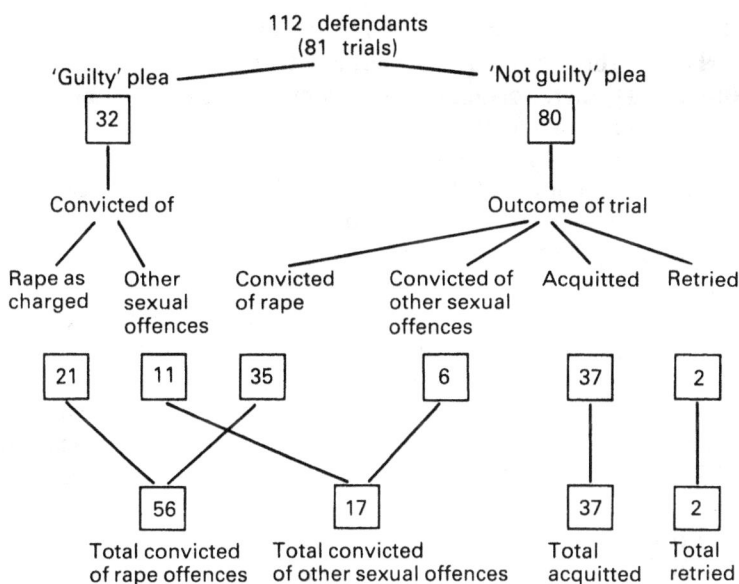

Figure 3.1: *Outcome of Old Bailey cases*

one defendant. Forty-three per cent of the accused were charged in conjunction with one or several other men. The majority of these multiple rapes involved three or more co-defendants. Men involved in multiple rapes in this sense almost invariably pleaded 'not guilty', with one exception where two defendants charged together admitted the offence in court. This was a somewhat unusual case, insofar as one of them was on parole from a nine-year sentence for robbery and rape, committed in almost identical circumstances some years earlier. The other was on licence from a seven-year sentence for burglary. Both defendants rather spec-tacularly resisted arrest, but subsequently made full statements to the police − the evidence against them was overwhelming. In sentencing them both to fifteen years in prison, the judge called for a public inquiry into the circumstances in which the men were released from prison. As he put it,

'I venture to think that no one who has examined the dreadful records that you have accumulated could fail to foresee what the consequences of setting you at liberty were going to be.'

In general, however, defendants involved in multiple rapes clearly feel that they have something to gain by pleading 'not guilty'. First, their version of the incident may gain credibility by the sheer force of repetition: when the jury have heard five men swear that the woman consented, and one woman swear that she did not, they are quite likely to be persuaded by the majority view. However, it would be wrong to imply that defendants involved in pair or group rapes always put up a united front. Far more often, they try to implicate their co-defendants while exonerating themselves, and the inconsistencies in accounts which emerge may actually favour the prosecution case. On the other hand, it is often difficult to prosecute successfully in such cases, particularly if the accused were strangers to the victim, as she may have difficulty in remembering and stating clearly in court just who did what at which precise stage. Any confusion on these issues is a veritable gift for the defence, as the following extract illustrates. This is taken from a trial where five youths were accused of raping a 14-year-old girl. She knew three of them vaguely, having attended the same school but the other two were complete strangers to her. Her evidence as to the order in which the boys had intercourse with her had been pretty consistent, until the fourth time she had to repeat this in cross-examination:

Victim: Joe was the second boy to have sexual intercourse with me. When I had sex with Phil, he [Joe] held my legs and then went out.
Defence counsel: That is not what you said before: you said that the boy with the glasses had intercourse with you after Joe.
Victim: It might have been, but I am not wrong about Joe helping in the next incident, and with Phil.
Defence counsel: But in your statement to the Magistrates' Court, you said that he left the room?
Judge: What impression is the jury supposed to get from this?

After a brief adjournment, the cross-examination continued:

Defence counsel: Would you agree that your evidence, as to the detail, hasn't been the same on each occasion?
Victim: I am somewhat confused as to the details.
Defence counsel: I suggest to you that Joe did not come back after leaving the bedroom.
Victim: He did.

Defence counsel: Yesterday was the first time you said that, wasn't it?
Victim: I can't remember. I don't know whether I've mentioned before
that Joe was holding me down during intercourse with Martin, the
second time. He wasn't there when I had intercourse with the last boy.
I don't remember when the third incident with Martin took place. I
don't remember whether I've mentioned it before.

As far as the number of victims was concerned, the majority of
trials involved only one woman or girl. Men accused of raping
more than one woman nearly always pleaded 'guilty', and they
formed a not insignificant proportion of all 'guilty' pleas: over a
third of those who admitted the offence had raped more than
one woman, usually on different occasions; the comparable figure
among those pleading 'not guilty' was 12 per cent. The most
likely explanation for this phenomenon is that the sheer weight of
evidence in cases involving several women considerably increases
the likelihood of a conviction. Where a man is charged with raping
four women unknown to one another on four separate occasions,
his chances of discrediting all of them at the trial are fairly remote
and it becomes much more difficult for him to produce a credible
account alleging consent on all occasions. Nevertheless, this is
certainly not impossible when smaller numbers of victims are
involved. One man, for example, was accused of raping two young
women on separate occasions several months apart. His modus
operandi had been almost identical: he met his victims, just arrived
from abroad, at a youth centre where they were looking for somewhere to stay. He offered them accommodation for a day or two,
with an apparently convincing story that he lived in a large house
with several other people. Both of them accepted his offer, and
subsequently made a rape complaint to the police. One of them
actually ran out into the street naked after his attack, crying and
sobbing hysterically, until a woman passer-by calmed her down
and called the police. The two women had never met before the
trial, indeed they came from different countries; both felt the need
to contact a Rape Crisis Centre; and both produced virtually
identical accounts of their experience with the accused during
the trial. However, the judge eventually directed that neither
complainant's story corroborated the other, and in the absence
of little or any other independent evidence, the defendant was
acquitted. Needless to say, his story had been that both incidents

took place with the women's consent.

Reported rapes in this sample appear to involve mainly young, single persons, both as victims and offenders, although defendants were marginally more likely to be married or cohabiting than were their victims in this particular sample. Just under a third of both defendants and victims were teenagers, with almost half of the defendants being under 25 at the time of committing the offence. The law does not allow boys under the age of 14 to be charged with rape: they can be convicted of aiding and abetting, but no more, even if there is undisputed evidence that they are the principal perpetrators of the full offence. This is because of an absurd but irrebuttable presumption that under this age, boys are incapable of sexual intercourse. The Criminal Law Revision Committee's 1984 Report on Sexual Offences[2] made a firm recommendation for the repeal of this provision, but for the time being, it remains unaltered.

The youngest offender in this study was just 14 when he raped two women at knifepoint on separate occasions, having already been convicted of an indecent assault some months previously. The youngest victim in the sample was 6 years old, and she had been assaulted by a neighbour who, at 61, was the oldest defendant. His statement to the police said that, despite his victim's extreme youth, the sexual activities between them occurred not only with her consent, but also with a good deal of active participation. His plea to 'guilty' to indecent assault, but 'not guilty' to rape, was accepted and he was sentenced to two years' imprisonment.

The oldest victim was 92 years old. She was brutally beaten and suffered fractures to her jaws, several ribs, cuts to her hands and arms, as well as appalling internal injuries at the hands of two teenage youths, one of whom also raped her. He denied attempted murder, but admitted rape and was heard whistling with relief when Mr Justice Melford-Stevenson, considered to be one of the toughest judges on the bench, sentenced him to four years' imprisonment.

One important and particularly enduring myth about rape is that it is an offence which generally involves people who were previously not known to each other. However, various American studies have found that between 39 per cent[3] and 68 per cent[4] of rape victims and offenders were to some degree known to one another. Closer to home, Wright's study of rape records considered genuine by the police in six English counties found a similarly high proportion of offences committed by men known to the victim. As he wrote,

Most of the attacks, whether committed by a lone man or a group of men, involved people who knew each other. In about 60 per cent of the assaults, the victim could name her assailant. Two-thirds of these cases involved relationships which could be described as 'close'. In the rest, the parties were briefly or superficially acquainted.[5]

According to the London Rape Crisis Centre, over 50 per cent of women who contact them have had some prior contact with the man who rapes them[6]. Such data refute the widely held myth that rapists are strangers to the women they rape, and are consistent with the findings of the present study where 60 per cent of the defendants were previously known to their victims. The type of existing relationship varied considerably. In some cases, the parties involved were general acquaintances, who may or may not have known each other's full names. This group included, for example, two adolescents who had been at the same school for some years, and knew each other by sight, and a victim who worked as a cashier in a garage where her would-be assailant was a regular customer. In other instances, the relationship was closer: one young woman complained of being raped by her brother's friend whom she had met at the family home on many occasions. The category also includes former girlfriends/boyfriends, and cases where the victim and the defendant lived in the same household (e.g. assaults by stepfathers).

Defendants who had been strangers to their victims were much more likely to plead 'guilty' than those who had known them previously. Fifty-three per cent of those pleading 'guilty' had raped strangers; the corresponding proportion among the 'not guilty' pleas was 34 per cent. It appears that defendants whose offence more closely approximates to the stereotype of the 'real' rape are more likely to be selected into the group that do not contest the charge. One possible explanation for this may be that in general, the weight of evidence against them is very strong, and it is very much more difficult for them to put forward a defence of consent with any credibility.

Another prevalent myth about rape is that an excellent way of avoiding it is not to venture outside unaccompanied after dark, or preferably ever in some areas. This too is firmly refuted by the findings of this study: 72 per cent of the rapes tried at the Old Bailey had been committed indoors, including a staggering 37 per cent in the victim's own home. Moreover, entry into the victim's home is very likely to have been elaborately planned well in advance. This strongly challenges the stereotype of the rapist who pounces in a dark alley after being sexually provoked by a reckless and glamorous female passer-by.

The trial process

Different procedures apply to the trial of men pleading 'guilty' and 'not guilty'. When a defendant admits the charge, he is usually sentenced almost immediately. There is no jury, and very little evidence is actually given in court. The victim does not have to appear at all. It is simply a matter of prosecution counsel outlining the circumstances of the offence, and calling evidence of the defendant's previous convictions, if any. Social inquiry and/or medical reports are sometimes presented to the Court. This is followed by a plea in mitigation by defence counsel, and the judge then sentences the defendant. The whole procedure is generally brief, and does not involve any of the complexities of a contested trial.

When the defendant pleads 'not guilty' to the offence or offences charged, a jury is empanelled to try him. In all criminal trials, the burden of proof rests with the prosecution, and in a rape case, this amounts to establishing a number of matters, one or more of which may be in dispute. These include showing that the right man is in the dock; that sexual intercourse took place between him and the woman in question at the relevant time; that the intercourse was without her consent; and that he knew that she was not consenting, or did not care whether she did or not. The standard of proof required is very high: before convicting, the jury must be sure that the accused did indeed commit the offence.

Counsel for the prosecution opens the case by telling the jury what the defendant is charged with, and by summarising the Crown case. Prosecution witnesses are then called to give their evidence. In a rape trial, the complainant is almost invariably the first witness. Evidence in chief is followed by cross-examination

for the defence, which is designed to '(a) . . . elicit evidence favourable to the defence case, and (b) to discredit the testimony of the
witness'.[7] It is usually just before or during cross-examination of
the woman that the defence makes an application to the judge, in
the absence of the jury, to question her about her previous sexual
experience.

The complainant's evidence is usually followed by that of a
medical witness, who talks about her condition after reporting
the offence. Police officers then generally give evidence of the
circumstances of the defendant's arrest, details of any interviews
with him, as well as details of written statements.

There may be other witnesses whose evidence completes the
case for the prosecution, and this is of course dependent on the
individual circumstances of each case. Statements of witnesses may
also be read out: this occurs when the prosecution introduces
evidence which is not disputed by the defence, such as, for example,
forensic evidence that sexual intercourse took place at the relevant
time between the victim and the defendant.

At the end of the prosecution case, the defence may apply to
the judge, in the absence of the jury, for a direction to acquit the
defendant. This can be done by arguing that the prosecution failed
to produce any evidence to establish some essential ingredient of
their offence, or that the evidence produced is so weak or discredited by cross-examination that no reasonable jury could
convict. If the application is successful, the defendant is acquitted
at this stage. If it is not, or if there is no such application, the trial
proceeds to the defence case. In a rape trial, the case for the defence
tends to be relatively brief and hinges on the defendant, who can
either decline to give evidence, or he can give it on oath like any
other witness[8]. If he does give evidence, he is subject to cross-
examination by the prosecution. There may be other defence
witnesses to establish, for example, an alibi for the defendant.

When all the evidence has been heard, prosecution and defence
counsel in turn address the jury about their respective cases.
Finally, the trial judge sums up the case and directs the jury about
the relevant law. In a rape trial, his directions include some
statement about the burden and standard of proof, the legal definition of rape and the main components of the offence. He also warns
the jury against the danger of convicting on the uncorroborated
evidence of the woman and tells them what evidence, if any, is

capable of constituting corroboration in the particular trial. After the summing-up, the jury retire to consider their verdict and if it is one of guilty, the court proceeds to sentence as in an uncontested trial.

The victim in a rape trial is the chief prosecution witness: without her evidence, the case against the defendant collapses. In fact, a fairly substantial number of men are acquitted if she is unwilling or unable to attend court, however legitimate the reasons for her absence. A case against four youths, for example, was dropped when the court was told that the 13-year-old complainant was no longer in the country; the date of the trial was fixed over a year after her initial complaint to the police, by which time she and her family had returned to the West Indies.

The time lapse between the reporting of a rape to the police and the trial can be considerable. A delay of around eight months is average, but some women may have to wait for as long as a year and a half before being called upon to appear in court. They may arrive there only to find that the trial date has been postponed. If the case goes ahead as scheduled, they will probably wait several hours outside the courtroom quite possibly sitting on the same bench as the defendant's relatives or friends who are also in court. Indeed, the defendant himself, if he is out on bail, may be passing by on his way in and out of court.

Once a woman gets into the witness box, she can expect to spend anything from one hour to several working days there – the average is somewhere between three and four hours. Most of that time will be spent in cross-examination. However, her ordeal begins with her evidence for the prosecution, which entails recounting every sexual detail of the rape incident. The following extract from one victim's evidence is typical of what may emerge at this stage:

'He tried to insert his penis – unsuccessfully at first, he was flaccid. He forced me to play with his penis. He had me pinned down on the floor. I was in extreme pain. He grabbed hold of my arm, and he pushed my hand down towards it. He finally managed to get an erection and he put his penis in my vagina. My right leg was under the car, and my left leg was turned up against the wall. He ejaculated inside me. He was telling me he loved me and in the same sentence he was telling me what a cow I was. He kept repeating that. Afterwards, he withdrew but he didn't get up.... Later, he pulled me up to my feet and said he wanted me again. He was still holding on to my wrists. He lay down – my back was towards the door. He started to pull me down on top of him – he said this time I want you on top of me.'

Apart from vividly bringing back painful memories, having to go through the incident in such explicit detail may just prove too much for some women. They may be unfamiliar with some of the sexual terminology involved, and find it inordinately difficult to convey what happened in the intimidating and formal setting of a court. Let us not forget that they are facing a judge, several barristers wearing wigs and gowns, and possibly another fifty or more total strangers, including reporters and members of the public. It is little wonder that some women in such circumstances find it virtually impossible to utter the words so desperately needed if there is to be any chance of a conviction. The following extract illustrates the problem for an 18-year-old youngster, whose assailant at the age of 21 had already served a three-year sentence for rape:

Victim: He did not believe me when I said I had a period. He laughed it off, he just kept trying.
Prosecution counsel: Trying what?
Victim: (No answer)
Prosecution counsel: Is it that you can't remember or that you're embarrassed?
Victim: (No answer, crying)
Prosecution counsel: Is it that you're embarrassed?
Victim: (No answer)
Prosecution counsel: He kept trying what?
Victim: (After a long silence) He just tried ... carried on ... in between my legs.

While some women, on the surface at least, appeared calm and reasonably able to cope with the court process, about half of them broke down in tears during their time in the witness box, and were temporarily unable to continue with their evidence. Some cried almost continuously, had difficulty getting words out, spoke almost inaudibly, and were visibly distressed by the whole procedure. They were anxious, nervous, tense, frightened, embarrassed – one victim, aged 21 at the time, was clutching a rag doll throughout her time in the witness box. A little girl of 11 experienced a total breakdown when she was asked to point out the man who attacked her – the following day, the court was informed that psychiatric treatment had to be arranged for her.

This part of the ordeal is, unfortunately, unavoidable. In any criminal trial, witnesses for the prosecution have to state their case against the defendant – rape is no exception, even if it does involve intimate and embarrassing matters for the complainant. The response of judges at this stage is crucial – they can do much to minimise or to magnify her ordeal. Some judges, while not actually hostile, seem to find the whole business almost as embarrassing as if they were in the witness box themselves, and do their utmost not to get involved. They might, for example, speak about the victim's distress and what might be done about it through a third party, usually prosecution counsel. Their attitude is best summed up as one of distaste and detachment. There is the odd judge who behaves appallingly and is downright aggressive when faced with a tearful and reluctant victim. On one occasion, a teenage victim was having great difficulty in telling the court about the sexual details of the rape – she became very upset, crying and muttering 'I can't, I can't say it'. The judge looked at the jury with some exasperation and brutally told her to pull herself together. Many judges are, however, sympathetic at this stage, particularly when the complainant is very young: cases are adjourned, glasses of water produced, the matron called for, the girl or woman is offered a chair. In one memorable case, the Recorder of London even went as far as to clear the public gallery in an attempt to create a less threatening atmosphere for the witness.

It is when it comes to the cross-examination of victims that rape trials begin to differ very sharply from trials of other criminal offences. It is often asserted that in most criminal cases, the credibility of the event is not an issue because of the unambiguous visible signs which indicate that a crime has taken place. When it comes to homicide, there is usually a body; burglary is generally accompanied by signs of forcible entry, malicious damage, and the disappearance of property. However, for many rapes all we have is signs of intercourse, possibly accompanied by some minor bruising, and a woman who says that she did not consent to the intercourse. There is no logic whatever in demanding a higher standard of proof in rape than in other crimes, yet this is precisely what is happening, if not in theory, certainly in practice. Evidence of intercourse and the woman's statement are rarely sufficient to establish that the offence has occurred. As Chambers argued,

Rape cases at the Old Bailey

The special circumstances of sexual assault incidents have made it very easy for accused persons to claim consent, indeed most accused persons in rape complaints, even when caught in the act or at the scene of the crime, do so. On account of this, complainers who would have been considered obvious victims in the circumstances of another crime have to do more to show evidence of a genuine assault[9].

Yet, as we have seen above, there is no evidence that bogus complaints are any more common for rape than for any other criminal offence. Indeed, it takes very little imagination to think of reasons why some might find it tempting to stage a burglary in their own homes, or to report a theft that never took place.

The defence at rape trials uses a number of strands of attack to undermine the woman's evidence and to shake her story, all of which would be considered totally unacceptable if she had reported, say, a serious non-sexual assault. First, there is continual questioning about the details of the rape, with suggestions that she was in the defendant's company willingly, that any protests she made were not genuine, that the intercourse was with her consent, and any injuries, the result of loveplay. A second strand is to probe her prior relationship, however vague or distant, with the accused, and on the strength of that, to suggest that she must have known what to expect when she accepted a lift, invited him in for a drink, allowed him in to read the gas meter, etc. A real trump card for the defence is a previous sexual relationship between her and the accused: once that is established, it will be practically impossible to convince the jury that the incident in question was anything other than one in a long series of consensual acts. In addition, her general character and reputation are probed in great detail: the list of less than 100 per cent 'respectable' women is almost endless, and includes Greenham Common supporters, single mothers, mothers with children in care, girls with punk hairstyles, women with a criminal record, or anyone living in a commune. This line of questioning is based on the assumption that such women are unlikely to be genuine victims of rape; or worse, that even if they are raped, it does not matter all that much.

Lastly, the woman's previous sexual experience with persons other than the defendant is used to suggest that because she has consented to intercourse with one or several other men in the past, she is that much more likely to have agreed to the defendant too.

53

These various strands of attack, as well as their impact on juries, will be discussed in greater detail in later chapters. Suffice it to say for the moment that cross-examination of this scope and nature of victims of any other crime would be unthinkable. An extract from a fictitious piece where the victim of a robbery, held up at gunpoint in the street, is questioned in the style of a rape cross-examination makes this point very well:

Mr Smith ... have you ever been held up before?
No.
Have you ever given money away?
Yes, of course.
And you did so willingly?
What are you getting at?
Well, let's put it like this, Mr Smith. You've given money away in the past. In fact, you have quite a reputation for philanthropy. How can we be sure that you weren't contriving to have your money taken from you by force? ... What time did this hold-up take place, Mr Smith?
About 11 pm.
You were out in the street at 11 pm? Doing what?
Just walking.
Just walking? You know that it's dangerous being out on the street that late at night? Weren't you aware that you could have been held up?
I hadn't thought about it.
What were you wearing at the time, Mr Smith?
Let's see ... a suit. Yes, a suit.
An expensive suit?
Well, yes, I'm a successful lawyer, you know.
In other words, Mr Smith, you were walking around the streets late at night in a suit that practically advertised the fact that you might be a good target for some easy money, isn't that so? I mean, if we didn't know better, Mr Smith, we might even think that you were asking for this to happen, mightn't we?[10]

One aspect of the cross-examination that rape victims were regularly subjected to has been ostensibly stopped or at least severely curtailed by the Sexual Offences (Amendment) Act 1976. Before discussing the application of the relevant section of that Act in court, the impact of the anonymity provision, both for victims and accused, will be considered. In an attempt to encourage more women to report rape, the 1976 legislation gave them protection from publicity, subject to certain exceptions. The following chapter will look at the ways in which the anonymity provisions have been implemented, discusses some of their unforeseen consequences, and points to areas where further change is needed.

Chapter 4

The limits of anonymity

———————◆———————

The victim

A study of the press coverage of rape cases in Britain over a period
of twenty years before 1976 found that 54 per cent of the reports
revealed the name of the victim, and a third also gave her address[1].
Details of the evidence and various discrediting remarks made to
her by defence counsel were also reported, although not as frequently as the authors expected. Although the authors found that
the quality of press stories did not actually deteriorate over the
period of study, the tremendous violation of privacy which results
from detailed reports has, probably rightly, been argued to be a
significant deterrent when it comes to women's willingness to make
a complaint of rape.

The Sexual Offences (Amendment) Act 1976 prohibits the publication and broadcasting of the name, and of any other material
likely to lead to the identification of, a woman as a complainant in
a rape case after a person has been accused of the offence. Any
proprietor, editor or publisher of a publication which infringes this
rule is liable to a fine of up to £500. A provision of this sort, it
will be remembered, was strongly advocated by the Heilbron
Group who felt that fear of publicity on the part of rape victims
was a major stumbling block when it came to reporting the offence.
As the Report spells out,

Even in the case of a wholly innocent victim whose assailant is convicted,
public knowledge of the indignity which she suffered in being raped may
be extremely distressing and even positively harmful, and the risk of
such public knowledge can operate as a severe deterrent to bringing
proceedings. Furthermore, since in a criminal trial guilt must be proved

to the satisfaction of the jury, an innocent victim can never be sure that a conviction will follow her complaint. If the accused is acquitted, the distress and harm caused to the victim can be further aggravated, and the danger of publicity following an acquittal can be a risk a victim is not prepared, understandably, to take.[2]

This view and the ensuing restrictions on publicity have attracted criticism on two fronts. It has been assumed, on the one hand, that the fact of anonymity increases the risk of false accusations (an assumption which has not been borne out by facts); and, on the other, that the proposition that anonymity would encourage women to report rape is at best dubious, particularly in smaller areas where their identity may well become common knowledge.

Geis and Geis base their main criticism on the argument that the anonymity provision implicitly endorses the basic assumptions and myths that have made rape such a 'special' criminal offence. The need for the victim's anonymity is based on the idea that there is something essentially different between victims of rape and those of other violent offences. The implication is that there is something shameful and stigmatising about rape, something which is likely to compromise a victim's character and reputation. While Geis and Geis agree that these assumptions 'have much basis in fact', they strongly argue that the right way forward is not through the endorsement of these notions by measures such as the protection of the victim's anonymity. As they put it,

The fight will be better fought by calm insistence that it is no different to be raped than to be victimized by other criminal offences. The incentive for such a campaign could be seriously undermined by the new anonymity provisions which push rape into a shadowy status.[3]

While it is difficult not to sympathise with the ideology embodied in this view, it fails to take account of the widespread concern that has developed in recent years over what is estimated to be very large numbers of unreported rapes, as well as over the plight of the rape victim who not only has to go through the trauma of giving evidence in a court of law, but also frequently has to suffer the additional ordeal of seeing detailed accounts of the most personal and intimate aspects of her evidence in the local, or indeed the national, press.

In any event, the victim's anonymity under the 1976 Act is far from total. First, it only starts at a relatively late stage: although the Heilbron Committee proposed that it should begin with the making of a complaint to the police, Parliament chose a later point, namely the appearance in court of a man charged with a rape offence. There is no logic in awaiting the date of a court appearance before ensuring that the victim's identity is kept secret. This is particularly relevant during the police investigation of the offence. As the Criminal Law Revision Committee recently noted, 'for a constable improperly to disclose information about a complaint of rape may render him liable to disciplinary proceedings'[4] – but not to prosecution under the 1976 Act.

This limitation has further, very disturbing, aspects. Over a period of a few months, two women were reported in the national press as having committed suicide shortly after reporting a rape, but before the start of any trial. They were both unequivocally identified. It would seem that anonymity is thought to be superfluous when the victim, for whose protection it was devised, is dead. There is no specific reference to such circumstances in the 1976 Act, but public interest does not demand the exact identification of victims so disturbed by the rape as to feel unable to face life any longer. There is also a strong argument to be made for the protection of the victims' families, particularly when young children are involved, as indeed they were in at least one of these cases.

A second important limitation of the anonymity provision is that it only applies to publications, broadcasts and similar material. It does not cover court proceedings. This, understandably, is a source of considerable anxiety to many women who are asked to identify themselves and state their address in court, in the presence of the defendant, as well as possibly his friends and family, not to mention a public gallery full of strangers. Rapists not infrequently threaten their victims with serious reprisals if they should report to the police and go through with the case. Of course, many of them know their victim's identity by the time they get to court: they may have known her before the rape; they may have broken into her home and raped her there; they may have stolen various belongings containing this information; or they may have seen it on her statement to the police. But some offenders do not know the precise identity of their victims and there is no reason why they should find out during the trial. This is undoubtedly an aspect of the court appearance which most victims find extremely distressing. One woman whose assailant, a total stranger, was sentenced only to a short term of imprisonment describes her fears:

He lived locally and I was very frightened it would happen again. . . . It was in the papers afterwards as well, but no names. That was my biggest worry, and I did insist with the police that if I went to court, then no one, you know, would know. But in fact it's very bad because they give out your name and address in court, and he was there. And that worried me, that really worried me, because I thought he can be just as quick noting that down in his memory, and that did worry me. I hadn't been aware of that until I got to court. I didn't mention it to the police afterwards, but I felt that was wrong.'[5]

Beyond being distressing and worrying for the victim, the conse-quences of such disclosures can be tragic. In 1985, a man just released from prison after serving a sentence for rape, who had threatened to kill his victim if she reported him, did just that.

The third problem is that the anonymity restriction can be lifted by a judge in certain circumstances. The defendant may apply to the court before the beginning of his trial to have the woman publicly identified if he can convince the judge of the following:

(a) that the direction is required for the purpose of inducing persons to come forward who are likely to be needed as witnesses at the trial; and
(b) that the conduct of the applicant's defence at the trial is likely to be substantially prejudiced if the direction is not given.[6]

A similar provision exists for persons who have been convicted of a rape offence and who have given notice of appeal against the conviction: they can also apply for the anonymity restriction on the victim to be lifted and in this instance the Court of Appeal may direct the publication of her name if it is satisfied that this is necessary to obtain evidence in support of the appeal and that the 'applicant is likely to suffer substantial injustice if the direction is not given'.[7]

Fears that judges would use their powers to lift the anonymity restriction on the victim when the defendant is acquitted where they believed that she had lied or made a false accusation appear so far to have been unfounded. There have to date been no reports of judges lifting the ban on their own initiative and only one case where the defendant made a successful application before the start of his trial to have the victim's name published.

That case was unusual in a number of respects. First, the defendant, Powell, described in some newspaper reports as a wealthy company director, was one of only two middle-class men charged with rape in this sample. Second, he had a number of convictions for obtaining pecuniary advantage, which in this case meant giving invalid cheques to prostitutes. Third, while awaiting trial on bail for this offence, he committed another rape for which he was subsequently also tried at the Central Criminal Court. Before the first trial, his counsel asked for the name of the victim to be 'given as much publicity as possible'[8], so that witnesses could come forward to support the defendant's allegation that she was a prostitute who specialised in offering herself for flagellation.

The undisputed fact that the victim was a prostitute would have been introduced by the prosecution at the trial and, in the unlikely event that the prosecution made no reference to it, the defence most certainly would have. In none of the cases of this study was evidence of prostitution kept from the jury, and it is most unlikely that such evidence would ever be excluded under the provisions of the 1976 Act. Although it is doubtful whether evidence of prostitution is necessarily relevant to the issue of consent, Powell certainly did not need to publicise the victim's name merely to show that she was a prostitute. Nevertheless, he was charged with rape as well as with assault occasioning actual bodily harm, and his attempt to publicise what in court was termed 'a special kind of rather attractive side show for clients who preferred it' arose from that lesser charge. Before agreeing to lift the publicity ban, the judge did remark that he had also to have regard to the victim's feelings, but Powell's counsel replied that the publicity could be argued to boost her trade potentially. It was perhaps rather naive of everyone concerned genuinely to expect witnesses to come forward to give evidence of their specific dealings with the victim under these circumstances or indeed to know a prostitute's real name. Not surprisingly, no such witnesses were produced at the trial. The judge's decision in this case was fiercely criticised by women's groups who interpreted it as the thin end of the wedge, but to date this fear also appears to have been unjustified. Since the 1976 Act, Powell has been the only defendant charged with rape to succeed in publicising the victim's name.

Another loophole is that a Crown Court judge at a rape trial may direct that the anonymity provision does not apply if he is satisfied that it would impose an unreasonable restriction on the reporting of the proceedings at the trial and that it is in the public interest to remove it. He is not empowered to do that, however, simply by virtue of the defendant's acquittal.

The provision under which a victim's name can be publicised, because keeping it secret would impose unreasonable reporting restrictions deemed to be against the public interest, has only been evoked successfully once, in a horrific and widely publicised case tried at Durham Crown Court in 1984. Many readers will remember the case of Hutchinson, who broke into a house during the night when everybody was asleep and having first stabbed to death three members of a family, went on to rape repeatedly the daughter of the household at knifepoint. He was eventually found guilty of these offences and sentenced to life imprisonment, but not before all the lurid details of his defence had made headlines for a solid week.

Newspapers reported only the murder charges during the committal hearings and made no reference to the rape: obviously, as the rape and murders took place on the same occasion any reference to the rape charge on a member of the murdered family would have easily identified their surviving daughter as the rape victim. At the trial, however, the Sheffield Newspaper Group applied to the judge to have the details of the rape disclosed. It argued that the details of the murder and the rape were inextricably bound up and that it was in the public interest to remove any restrictions on publication. The case would be unreportable, it was said, if the central characters could not be named. Although the application was opposed by lawyers representing the victim, the judge granted the newspapers' request and allowed both Hutchinson and the victim to be identified. As if that were not bad enough, many of the national dailies went a lot further than merely to name the girl involved. *The Times*, for example, usually among the more restrained papers, published the same photograph of her twice within a week. Worse still, most newspapers provided a verbatim account of the more sordid parts of her cross-examination where the defence alleged that she was the one who invited him to the house and that she was a willing party to the intercourse. The *Observer* strongly opposed the disclosure of the victim's name and details of her evidence, arguing that in this case, discretion should have prevailed:

The interests of justice and decency might have been better served by reporting only the outcome of the case. There was nothing in last week's proceedings which could not have been kept until the jury had reached its verdict . . . the newspapers could have reported the matter in as much detail as public scrutiny really requires.[9]

For the victim in that case, reliving her ordeal in the full glare of publicity, with the particular line of questioning pursued, must have been one of the most devastating experiences that one can imagine any victim suffering in a British court. It is also an experience which must not be allowed to happen again and this can only be ensured by the removal of any scope for judicial discretion in this area. However, Stuart Bell MP's call to tighten up the law in this respect received the cold shoulder from the Home Secretary who, while sympathising with the plight of this particular victim, had confidence in the existing arrangements and felt that it was right to preserve some discretion in this area.

There have been no legal cases claiming a breach of the law on the anonymity of the victim and only one complaint to the Press Council about a report which appeared in the *East London Advertiser*. In that instance, the victim was not named but the Press Council took the view that the report would have led to the identification of the woman in the area where the paper was published. In upholding the complaint, the Council noted:

It is accepted by all newspapers that they do not identify victims in cases of this kind. In this instance the description of the victim given in the newspaper would clearly identify her to people in the circles in which she moved and was perhaps more objectionable than identification by name to people who were not known to her.[10]

So, newspaper publishers and broadcasters appear to conform to Section 4 of the 1976 Act. Nevertheless, it may be argued that the Act has not gone far enough and that the privacy of victims may still be threatened by the publication of various details such as their age, nationality, where they work or live, etc. Women may be referred to as Miss X in these reports, but at times their authentic initials are used. It is hardly a matter of national importance that a rape victim is a widowed academic, a prostitute, a schoolgirl or a Tory MP's daughter. Details such as these, in combination with extracts from the evidence presented at a trial, may identify victims at least in the local community which is precisely where they would most want to avoid publicity. It is unlikely that cases of this sort would be reported to bodies like the Press Council.

Advocates of the 1976 reforms hoped that apart from ensuring the rape victim's anonymity, the new provisions would also alter the quantity and, above all, the quality of press reports relating to rape. Hay, Soothill and Walby have monitored the impact of the legislation on press reports of rape and, somewhat surprisingly, found that despite attempts at control, rape reporting had dramatically increased.[11] As far as quality is concerned, with the Act potentially reducing the amount of evidence available about the woman's sexual past, it was hoped that newspapers would no longer have the necessary raw material for the sort of titillating rape reports which had been so prevalent before 1976, and that they would therefore lose interest in the subject. Nevertheless, the press continues to report rape in the sensationalised form which has been strongly criticised for many years now. The London Rape Crisis Centre's 1982 Report states that rape

is a newspaper and magazine seller, a headline maker, a subject guaranteed to increase listening and viewing audiences.... We have found that violence against women is frequently glorified by the media whilst the real suffering of women is dismissed or ignored.[12]

The study of newspaper reports of rape referred to above makes a similar point and argues that rape reports may be seen as part of a sexually titillating package used to sell newspapers. In particular, the authors found that the selection of rape cases published in the *Sun* and the *News of the World* were clearly determined by marketing considerations:

These two newspapers – owned by the same person, Rupert Murdoch – have the widest coverage of rape cases. In 1978, there were seventy-two reports in the *News of the World*, and thirty-two in the *Sun*. But, remarkably, not one rape case in that year was covered by both newpapers. The possibility of this happening by chance is so remote as to defy calculation.... From this kind of evidence, we suspect that the press is increasingly using the soft pornography of rape reports, and reports of other sex crimes, as a mechanism to sell newspapers.[13]

The defendant

Anonymity for persons accused of rape was considered but rejected by the Advisory Group on the Law of Rape. Nevertheless, the clause covering this matter was introduced during the Committee Stage of the Sexual Offences (Amendment) Bill. Some MPs felt that it was 'intolerable' for the victim to be given anonymity while the defendant did not enjoy a similar privilege. The House of Commons rejected the Heilbron Committee's view that comparisons and parallels should not be drawn between victim and accused, but rather between persons accused of rape and those accused of other offences. The granting of anonymity for the victim alone was thought to be a dangerous course of action, which would mean that

someone who brings a completely groundless and, perhaps, malicious accusation of rape can be protected both from the social disapproval of the community and, in most cases ... from other redress at the hands of the unfortunate defendant, while the defendant's name can be stigmatised even if he is fully acquitted.[14]

It was also argued that rape is not only a 'special' offence for the victim, but that it carries unique elements for the defendant too. The stigma of being unjustly accused of rape was such that

an acquittal ... is not enough finally and thoroughly to clear a man's name and cleanse his character. There will always be those in the community and at work who are taking decisions about career prospects of the man who will say 'No smoke without fire', and that can be most damaging to the individual.[15]

These arguments, despite some opposition, convinced the majority of the House of Commons and the Sexual Offences (Amendment) Act 1976 protects the defendant from publicity until he has been convicted of the offence. However, if the accused person himself applies either to a Magistrates' Court before his trial, or to the Crown Court during his trial, to have this restriction lifted the Court may direct that the anonymity clause should not apply. The Court may also do this if it feels that anonymity would impose a substantial and unreasonable restriction on the reporting of the trial proceedings.

An accused person's co-defendant may also apply for the anonymity provision to be lifted under circumstances similar to those which apply to the publication of the victim's name, i.e. where witnesses are needed to come forward and where his defence would be prejudiced if his co-defendant's name were not publicised.

Outside Parliament, extending anonymity to defendants has been strongly criticised, as most commentators felt that the Heilbron Group's approach had been right in principle:

Anonymity for the individual accused of rape, it appears obvious, stems from sympathy with the possible woes of the 'respectable' person who is accused of the crime. Surely, Parliament has in mind a situation such as one in which a female of dubious repute accuses a well-positioned male – a Judge, a prominent businessman, or an MP, for instance – of having sexually assaulted her. Certainly, they were not much concerned with the reputations of all falsely accused persons – otherwise, they would have seen the illogic of protecting the accused rapist from publicity while exposing the improperly accused burglar or robber to equally unwanted attention.[16]

As with the victim, the anonymity provision for the defendant is 'working' insofar as there have been no prosecutions of newspaper publishers or editors to date under Section 6 of the 1976 Act. There has only been one case where the defendant's name has been published on his own initiative after his acquittal had been legitimated, as it were, when another man confessed to the crime he had been initially charged with.

It is extremely rare for judges to allow the accused's identity to be revealed after a rape acquittal, even when the person concerned is convicted of another offence charged in the same indictment. One notable exception was a direction by Mr Justice Wien that the names of twin brothers acquitted of rape but convicted of unlawful imprisonment and assault charges should be published. He is reported as justifying this as follows:

The editor would be placed in an impossible situation if he was not free to publish as he thought fit in this case. Although both defendants have been acquitted of rape, I think it is in the public interest that he should feel free to publish, otherwise there will be an undue fetter on the press and there are too many fetters on the press at the moment.[17]

One unanticipated and very unfortunate effect of the anonymity provision for defendants has been that persons acquitted of rape but convicted of other charges arising from the same incident have, almost invariably, remained anonymous. Although few such cases have come to light, concern has been expressed about this phenomenon which is in breach of the fundamental principle that the identity of people who lose their liberty should be revealed. As an editorial in *Justice of the Peace* commented,

The Justices' Clerks' Society were surely right in their plea to the Government that no further restrictions should be placed upon the press without a comprehensive review of the existing law, the anomalies to which it can give rise and an attempt to balance the public interest in truthful and full reporting of criminal proceedings against the possible distress to which it can sometimes give rise.[18]

Findings from this study suggest that this phenomenon may be of considerable magnitude: almost 20 per cent of the defendants acquitted of a rape charge were nevertheless convicted of other offences. This was particularly likely to happen with defendants pleading 'guilty' to a lesser offence than rape. The charges these men were convicted of include a variety of offences from indecent assault, the most common category, to unlawful sexual intercourse, gross indecency, unlawful imprisonment, buggery and incest as well as the whole gamut of offences involving assault. It is in fact something of a misnomer to call these 'lesser' offences: with one exception, all these persons were sentenced to immediate imprisonment and over half of them received terms of over two years.

Of the nineteen defendants involved here, only one was identified in the press. He pleaded 'not guilty' to rape, but 'guilty' to unlawful sexual intercourse with a girl of 10, and this plea was accepted by the Crown. It was probably no accident that he received an extremely long sentence and that he had a string of convictions for similar offences. In the past, he had been sentenced to seven years for indecently assaulting a number of girls between the ages of 5 and 14. The offence he was charged with in this instance was committed about a year after he had been released on licence from that sentence. The judge deemed him 'a menace to little girls' and although he did not lift the anonymity restriction under Section 6, it was clear from his comments on sentencing that he had a message for the press to convey:

'The only thing I can think of in your favour is that you may have been encouraged by the intemperate benevolence of those who released you on parole, probably the Home Secretary of the day or his advisors.'

Under the circumstances, nobody seemed to object to the identification of this particular defendant. However, there is a major issue involved here: it is hard to justify the anonymity of the perpetrators of some very serious offences indeed by virtue of their (sometimes technical) acquittal of a rape charge. This anomaly highlights once again the imperative of reforming rape law in the context of the rest of criminal law, and particularly of not creating a fundamental distinction between offences which, for all intents and purposes, are extremely similar. It cannot be argued with any credibility that the dividing line between attempted rape and indecent assault, for example, in terms of the damage they may inflict on the victim or indeed in terms of the defendant's intent, is a very clear or important one.

Critics of this section of the Sexual Offences (Amendment) Act 1976 appear to have been vindicated. There was little justification in the first place for defendants and victims in rape cases to be treated in the same way with regard to anonymity. As has rightly been observed, there is no logic in arguing that being accused and acquitted of rape is any more damaging or stigmatising to the person involved than being similarly charged with murder or armed robbery. The implications of this anomaly have been compounded by its unforeseen impact on the identification of persons acquitted of rape but convicted of other offences which may be equally, if not more, serious. The Criminal Law Revision Committee's Report on Sexual Offences which was published in April 1984 recognises that anonymity for defendants in rape cases is an anomaly and recommends that the provision be repealed. It can only be hoped that legislative action will follow this proposal in the near future.

Anonymity was only one of the reforms introduced by the

Sexual Offences (Amendment) Act 1976 in an effort to afford greater protection for the victims of rape. The next chapter will discuss the effects of the provision which limits the admissibility of sexual history evidence and examine the nature of judicial decision-making in this area.

Chapter 5

As his Lordship pleases

No systematic study has ever been made of the type of sexual history evidence routinely admitted in rape trials before the advent of the 1976 Act. However, it is common knowledge that cross-examination on this issue, often extremely painful and distressing for the woman, was widespread. This is mainly what convinced the Advisory Group on the Law of Rape to recommend drastic changes in this area. Case law relating to this problem, however, is revealing. Before embarking on a discussion of the effect of legislative change on courtroom practice, therefore, the context in which the admission of evidence of the victims' sexual history became standard procedure in rape cases will be examined.

Sexual history then ...

A reading of case law indicates that evidence of the woman's sexual past with persons other than the defendant tended to fall into two major categories: first, that she was notoriously immoral, and second, that she had previously had sexual contact with someone other than the defendant.

Evidence of 'notorious bad character', usually a euphemism for an allegation of prostitution, was admissible because, so the argument went, that sort of background makes a woman more likely to consent to intercourse in general and with the accused in particular. The relevance of this kind of evidence to consent has been firmly entrenched in common law since an 1817 case, where the defence produced evidence of the victim's 'abandoned character' and 'lack of chastity'.[1] This rule, over the years, has allowed defence lawyers to question women in rape cases about a wide range of issues with a view to blackening their sexual reputation. In 1829,[2] a woman was asked whether she had been 'walking in the High Street, in Oxford, to look out for men,' and in 1843,[3] a 12-year-old girl was cross-examined about 'facts of indecency ... and of solicitation by her previously made to men to have connection with her'; and evidence was admitted in a trial in 1851,[4] that the victim had been seen twenty years earlier 'on the streets of Shrewsbury as a reputed prostitute'.

The principles embodied in the above cases have been followed in this century, and the pre-1976 position has been summarised as follows:

In a case other than rape, such evidence would clearly not be admissible. In rape cases, however, special rules applied. It was certain that evidence of intercourse with named men could not be admissible in a rape case, but evidence that the woman was a prostitute or, as in this case, that she was a woman of loose character and notorious for want of chastity or decency was, on the authorities, admissible.[5]

The second category of evidence relating to sexual experience involves what has been termed the woman's private sexual history which means any sexual relationships she may have had with persons other than the defendant, but excludes prostitution or 'bad reputation'. The earliest authority on this is interesting because it seems to establish that such evidence is not actually a proper matter for cross-examination. The judge in R v Hodgson (1812) held that 'the witness was not bound to answer these questions as they tended to incriminate and disgrace herself ... he [the judge] thought there was not any exception in the case of rape'.[6]

However, this case is hardly mentioned in later authorities except as an obsolete rule and other judges since have consistently held that the complainant could indeed be cross-examined as to particular acts of sexual intercourse with third parties. According to the Heilbron Report, various cases have also established that this was not because of its relevance to consent; rather, it was admissible as going to the credibility of the witness.

This appears to draw a clear, if somewhat odd, distinction in law between evidence of 'bad reputation' and private sexual history and has had far-reaching consequences for the way in which the relevance of sexual history evidence has been defined and interpreted. As mentioned above, evidence to show that the victim was, for example, a prostitute, had been admitted because it was felt to affect the issue of consent, as showing her as a person more likely to consent to sexual intercourse. However, evidence of private sexual history was in general differently justified: it was said to be relevant not to the issue in the trial, but to her credibility as a witness. The extraordinary assumption underlying this position is that the fact that a woman has had some sexual experience tends to show that she is an untruthful or unreliable witness.

Different rules of evidence apply to cross-examination to the issue in the trial (usually consent, in this instance) and to credit. The technicalities involved will not be discussed here in detail, except to stress the point that the distinction between the two types of sexual history evidence in rape trials is, to say the least, extremely nebulous. It is far from obvious whether a particular piece of evidence comes under the heading of 'notorious bad character' or private sexual history. Expressions such as 'lack of chastity', 'immorality' and 'promiscuity', for example, are used in this context whether it is the woman's lack of consent or general reputation that is being questioned. Moreover, if it is alleged that the victim has some sexual experience, she may ostensibly be cross-examined to credit, but the evidence introduced is bound to affect the jury's view of her likelihood to consent. As one commentator put it,

Here the difficulty is extreme for the jury might be excused if they thought that the prosecutrix's promiscuity had substantially more bearing on whether she consented than on whether she was a liar.[7]

In any event, it is clear that from the early nineteenth century to 1976, the victim in a rape trial was frequently exposed to a whole barrage of questions totally unrelated to the charge which aimed to discredit her evidence by suggesting, more or less explicitly, that she was the type of person who tends to consent freely. This clearly suggests that there is assumed to be a strong link between a woman's past sexual experience and her consent to sexual intercourse on the occasion of the rape incident. Her credibility as a rape victim is seen as dependent on her previous sexual conduct with persons other than the defendant. The rationale underlying the relevance of such evidence is based on the assumption that any degree of sexual experience in a woman is indicative

71

of an overall willingness to consent. In other words, it is thought more likely that an 'unchaste' woman would consent than a 'virtuous' one. At one extreme, attitudes to prostitution provide a good example of this view. The very fact that a woman is a prostitute tends to destroy her credibility as a rape victim, and this is clearly acknowledged in court: even contemporary judges warn juries, albeit in somewhat ambiguous terms, not to dismiss such cases out of hand:

'When one ... is considering thoughts about morality and immorality and permissive societies and all the rest of it, it is no excuse, even if that woman was a common prostitute, if she did not consent to intercourse and a man had intercourse with her against her will. Even with that sort of a woman, that is rape just the same.'

The Heilbron Group's approach constitutes a radical challenge to such assumptions arguing as it does that whatever a woman's sexual experience with partners of her choice, it cannot logically be construed as a general willingness to consent to sexual intercourse or as an indication of untruthfulness. It recommended, as we saw, that such evidence should no longer be introduced, save in exceptional circumstances. According to Section 2 of the Sexual Offences (Amendment) Act, an application must be made to the judge in the absence of the jury to introduce evidence or to cross-examine a victim about her sexual experience with any person other than the defendant. While, on the face of it, the Act appears to overrule the precedents established in the nineteenth century, it also seems to leave a good deal to the trial judge's discretion. In this respect, legislation is set out in very general terms. Section 2 goes no further than to say that

On such application, the judge shall give leave if and only if he is satisfied that it would be unfair to that defendant to refuse to allow the evidence to be adduced or the question to be asked.

In view of the broad discretionary legislation adopted here, there is a very real possibility that the absence of specific guidelines will lead judges to incorporate the assumptions reflected in nineteenth-century case law into their interpretation of the new Act. Just how is this section interpreted in court?

... and now

Of the fifty contested Old Bailey trials in this study, five failed to go ahead, usually because the victim was unable to give evidence. Applications for permission to introduce evidence of the woman's previous sexual experience were made in eighteen of the remaining forty-five contested trials (40 per cent) on behalf of twenty-nine defendants. They were most common in trials involving several defendants: 23 per cent of defendants tried alone made an application compared to 46 per cent of those involved in multiple rapes. The reason for this is probably that it becomes imperative to attack the woman's sexual morality when she is said to have agreed to intercourse with several men – the jury is unlikely to believe that of just anybody. Although in these cases, applications were not always made on behalf of all defendants, the introduction of evidence about the woman's sexual past has a halo effect, which affords some benefit to all concerned. When a judge allows cross-examination for one defendant, his co-defendants will also gain advantage from the fact that the jury is led to take a particular view of the victim's character. As one judge trying two men remarked, 'One can't help observing that if I allow one, the other will benefit.'

Predictably, the overwhelming majority of applications were made by defendants whose case involved the question of consent: nearly 60 per cent of these men wanted to bring in some evidence of the woman's sexual past. Applications under Section 2, although not universal, are certainly a good deal less exceptional than the Heilbron Group or Parliament intended. Furthermore, at 75 per cent, their success rate is considerable.

Applications under Section 2 were based on an interesting variety of grounds, although these were not always clearly distinguishable from their substance. In some cases, they were made without any attempt to argue the relevance of the proposed questions to the case. While judges generally intervened and required an explicit statement of the purpose of those questions, they occasionally allowed cross-examination to go ahead despite an open acknowledgment by all that the matters covered were irrelevant to the case:

Defence counsel: I want to cross-examine the complainant on her previous sexual experience. In her statement to the police, there is a sentence

which reads 'I am not inexperienced in matters sexual.' That is all I
seek to put to her.

Judge: I suppose that has not much to do with this case. I don't think
it's right to stop the question.

Generally, though, applications are a great deal more detailed and
the proposed cross-examination may be argued to be relevant to
the victim's credibility, to an issue in the trial excluding consent
and to the issue of consent.

The defence sought to introduce evidence of sexual history
because of its relevance to the victim's credibility in two circumstances: first, if there was an inconsistency between her evidence at the trial and her written statement to the police; and
second, if she had made one or more previous rape complaints.

An example of the first variety is a case where the victim's
statement included a reference to the last occasion when she had
intercourse before the rape. In her evidence at the trial, however,
she volunteered the information that she had in fact not had any
sexual experience beforehand. The medical evidence agreed with
her initial statement and the defence application was based on the
issue of her overall credibility as a witness: 'If she is lying about
her prior sexual experience, what else is she lying about?' The
judge allowed her to be cross-examined on this limited point. In
fact, a Section 2 application was only made as a matter of formality
because the victim had been caught out telling a lie and the lie
happened to concern her sexual history. Any major contradiction
of this sort between a witness's evidence and his or her written
statement would be forcefully underlined for the jury in any
criminal trial.

Inquiry into previous complaints of rape, the second category
here, is based on one of the most persistent themes in the history
of the offence – the fear of the false accusation. The fear may be
that the woman in question has a tendency to invent incidents of
rape which have no basis in reality or, alternatively, that she agrees
to sex only to label it as rape later on out of malice, embarrassment,
spite, jealousy or some other unworthy motivation. As one defence
counsel helpfully explained,

'Very often, there are people who allege rape for some psychological
reason. It may be some sexual fantasy. There is a certain kind of woman

74

who alleges rape, a certain type.... There is a type of woman who will make hysterical, untrue allegations of rape.'

In view of the deep suspicion with which the law has always treated women complaining of rape, it is hardly surprising that someone who has done so on more than one occasion is subject to extreme scrutiny.

The other assumption which comes into play is that several sexual assaults in the life of one woman are so improbable as to be virtually impossible. Consequently, all such allegations stand or fall together:

Judge: You want to tell the jury that three rapes in one year are so unlikely that she is not credible in this instance.
Defence counsel: I want to tell the jury that they should either believe all or none of her allegations.

Some applications under Section 2 were made in cases where there was a dispute as to the identity of the victim's sexual partner at the material time. This arises when the medical and/or forensic evidence shows that she did have sexual intercourse when she says she did, but the defendant denies that he was responsible. An application in such cases is then made to cross-examine about her sexual experience in order to offer an alternative interpretation of the scientific evidence – in other words, to suggest that she actually had sex with someone else at the time in question. As the Court of Appeal has stated, the reason for an application in these cases is obvious:

If no rape, and no emission has taken place, if none of these youths in other words had had an emission at the time of these alleged offences, then some other reason for the undoubted scientific finding of the presence of semen must be sought and the other possibility obviously was that this girl had had sexual intercourse with someone else previously, which would have accounted for the presence of human semen found upon her.[8]

Few would dispute that in such a case cross-examination about this limited point should be allowed, as it invariably is. Occasionally, however, defence counsel tries to pursue matters further, usually in the absence of any concrete instructions from their client. In one case concerning six youths who admitted being in the same room as the victim in various states of undress and engaging in a variety of sexual acts, but all denied penetration, the application went on:

Defence counsel: I would like to go further, and do a bit of probing in the normal way.
Judge: No. What do you mean, probing?
Defence counsel: Asking how often she was having sexual intercourse at the time, with whom. . .

Although further questioning along such lines was not permitted in any of these cases, there is an additional problem concerning this area. Nothing in Section 2 limits cross-examination on this point to cases where the main issue is the identity of the defendant or the occurrence of sexual intercourse. In one case, for example, where the defence was consent, defence counsel applied to bring in evidence of the victim's recent sexual past as follows:

'The defendant wore a contraceptive and there should not have been any semen in the complainant where in fact there was. The only explanation is that she had sexual intercourse with another man that evening.'

The application was successful, but it was not clear why. Was it that the victim was thought to be more likely to have consented to the defendant if she had had sexual intercourse with her boy-friend in the near enough past for semen still to be present? Or was it that someone else may have raped her, after which she willingly had intercourse with the defendant, only to accuse him of rape? Or was it some other equally tenuous explanation? As the trial unfolded, none of these lines was pursued and it is tempting to conclude that the cross-examination was entirely aimed at pre-judicing the jury against the victim.

The vast majority of applications were based on the argument that specific areas of the victim's sexual history were relevant to the issue of consent. This is the critical area for assessing whether the new Act has brought about any fundamental change in the trial of rape offences, and raises important questions about the meaning of relevance in this area. The Heilbron Group, as we have seen, felt that evidence of sexual history 'was rarely likely to be relevant to issues directly before the jury'. Although their approach has been accepted by Parliament in principle, the findings of this study suggest that judges' decision-making in this area continues to reflect the principles of case law established in the nineteenth century. The basic assumption that a victim's prior sexual experience is relevant in establishing consent has not been substantially altered by a procedural change in the law.

One measure of the importance of a 'good reputation' for a rape victim is the extent to which her prior virginity is used to strengthen the prosecution case. Women with no previous experience tend to be presented as highly trustworthy with regard to their complaint of rape. The prosecution inevitably introduce this in opening the case; later, the victim is asked about it; and finally, the doctor is questioned in some detail about the results of his examination. In other words, wherever possible, a victim's prior virginity is firmly underlined for the jury and, as we shall see below, this appears to contribute strongly to her credibility at the trial.

A further indication of the importance of virginity is the way in which the defence sometimes disputes the prosecution's allegation that the victim had had no sexual experience. In such cases, the issue takes on tremendous proportions and a good deal of time and effort is devoted by both sides in trying to make their version of the truth prevail or, as far as the defence is concerned, to sow some doubt at least in the minds of the jury. In one case, for example, the doctor's cross-examination went as follows:

Defence counsel: About the condition of the hymen, what does your examination mean?

Doctor: There was a single split in it, which had no connection with this incident.

Defence counsel: Can your examination show that she had not had sexual intercourse before that occasion?

Doctor: Yes, there would be more damage to the hymen.

Defence counsel: Once a woman has become used to sexual intercourse, you can't really tell?

Doctor: I would not say that this young lady was accustomed to frequent sexual intercourse. I would say her hymen was consistent with her being a virgin.

Defence counsel: If I suggest that the lady had sexual intercourse more than ten times about six months before this incident, is that consistent with your findings?

77

Doctor: I suppose it is possible. But I would have expected something different in the hymen if that had been the case.

In three trials, victims aged between 14 and 17 had not been virgins before the rape incidents and, in all cases, this became the substance of an application under Section 2 of the Act. It was argued that the jury should not deliberate on the assumption that the victim had been a virgin:

Defence counsel: The defence is consent, and this is relevant to establish consent: the fact that this was not the complainant's first experience of sexual intercourse. If it were, it would be heavily against the defendant. The matter ought to be before the jury, or, in view of her age, they may draw inaccurate conclusions about her virginity.

The implicit justification for that application is that because the victim had consented once, this made her more likely to consent again, even though different persons and circumstances were involved. As the judge in a similar case questioned,

'Are you saying that a girl of 15 who has had sexual intercourse before is necessarily more likely to consent, lie on the filthy ground and have sexual intercourse with complete strangers?'

The proposed questions in other applications may go further to suggest a greater degree of sexual experience, all in an effort to imply consent. For example:

Defence counsel: The defence is effectively that she invited [the two defendants] in a threesome on the bed. That kind of suggestion has to be balanced against the fact that she has had sexual experience and against the degree or extent of that experience.

In a similar vein, she may be asked about the number of sexual partners she has had, about her use of contraceptives and her gynaecological history.

In other cases again, Section 2 applications rely more explicitly on some notion of similarity between the victim's sexual experience and the circumstances of the rape that she is alleging. One way of doing this is to suggest that not only was she experienced, but that her sexual relationships had involved persons bearing some superficial similarity to the defendant. In one case, for example, two men in their forties were charged with the rape of a teenager, and the defence asked to cross-examine her in these terms:

'She was living with a man much older than herself. There was also another [older] man sharing their squat. I want to ask her about that.'

The implicit suggestion here was that because the victim had been cohabiting with an older man, she was more likely to consent to intercourse with others in that age group, including presumably the defendants. Elsewhere, the same line of reasoning was used with respect to race. In this case, the victim was white, her assailants black, and the defence had this to say:

'I want to show that the complainant was not averse to having sexual intercourse with coloured men. The jury should have no presumption of lack of consent because of the colour of the people involved here. Her sexual experience was almost entirely with coloured men.'

The racist assumptions this application reflects, incidentally, are not exclusive to the courts – during the debates of the Sexual Offences (Amendment) Bill, one MP defended the admissibility of such evidence on the grounds that it was important to know whether the victim was a girl who 'went' with black men or not: 'Let us face it', he said, on the basis of one knows not what experience, 'most white girls do not go to bed with coloured men.'[9]

Another approach is to suggest that the victim previously participated in the kind of sexual activity which also occurred between her and the defendant. Applications to cross-examine in this area almost invariably involve behaviour amounting to something more than sexual intercourse with one partner or, as some legal terminology has it, 'unnatural' sexual practices. An example is a case where the defendant claimed that his victim had asked him to have anal intercourse with her. Defence counsel wanted to cross-examine about previous incidents of anal sex with her boyfriend:

'The suggestion is that she had done that with her boyfriend regularly.... The girl, although a virgin, was not sexually inexperienced. She made suggestions to the defendant which are entirely incompatible with her account of struggles. In the course of sex play with her boyfriend, they had tried to have sexual intercourse.'

Finally, defence applications may be concerned with introducing evidence of what has been termed 'bad reputation', 'promiscuity' or prostitution. What is presented as consent to more than one or two persons is then interpreted as equating with indiscriminate consent. In one case, for example, the defendant had this to say:

'There had been previous occasions of sexual intercourse at the flat. We had gone there with Simon, Charlie, Kelly, the victim and me. I went up to bed with Kelly, I got up and when I came back, the complainant was in bed with Kelly, making advances to her. Kelly got up and went into the lounge. Then I had sexual intercourse with the complainant in the bedroom. Later, Charlie went into the bedroom with the complainant. He came out, and Simon went in then. He ended up staying the night. I think Charlie slept in the same room. I slept with Kelly. A week after that there was a similar occasion. I never actually saw her have intercourse with anyone, but Charlie and Jim spent time alone with her.'

Evidence of prostitution is invariably introduced in some way, usually without recourse to the 1976 Act, as being relevant to the case even when it is not part of the accused's story that he was to have paid for the victim's services. However, allegations of prostitution may also be made following a Section 2 application against victims who are clearly not prostitutes. For example, defence counsel in one case suggested that the complainant was a prostitute who only cried rape because she was upset by the financial arrangements (the details of which were not revealed) and because no sexual intercourse had actually taken place. The victim strongly denied this. At the defendant's retrial, the matter of prostitution was not mentioned at all. Another woman, a student nurse who first came into contact with the defendant in a part of town frequented by prostitutes, was also accused of being one herself, although again it was not part of the defendant's case that there was any business transaction between them.

Where the victim admits that she is a prostitute, the matter is likely to be aired in a great deal of detail in court. In one case, the judge was unable to contain his rather unhealthy curiosity and asked a prostitute a series of intrusive, prurient and totally irrelevant questions. He inquired, for example, as to whether she worked alone or with another woman, how long she had been a prostitute, who was managing her, at what stage of the transaction she got paid, how much and whether she had ever had a sexually transmitted disease.

Judges rule

Although judges received little guidance from Parliament on how to interpret Section 2, a very limited amount of case law had emerged by the time this study was carried out, and judges did consider this in coming to their decision in particular cases. The leading light was the case of R v Lawrence (1977), and this was referred to on a number of occasions. The Lawrence case decided that before allowing cross-examination about sexual history, the judge

must take the view that it is more likely than not that the particular question or line of cross-examination [if allowed] might reasonably lead the jury [properly directed in the summing up] to take a different view of the complainant's evidence.[10]

It is of course probable that any sexual experience in a victim which is capable of being construed as inappropriate will lead the jury to take not only a different, but also a considerably less favourable, view of her evidence. As the Heilbron Group commented, the jury

may react critically to any admissions that she may make on the assumption that any sexual experience, however unrelated to the charge, shows her to be a person more likely to consent to sexual intercourse, even with a stranger.[11]

The decision in Lawrence implicitly endorses that assumption and as such is most unhelpful as an interpretation of Section 2. Needless to say, it was extensively used as an argument in support of the admissibility of sexual history evidence in a number of rather dubious instances.

While High Court judges sitting at the Old Bailey had a degree of experience in dealing with applications under Section 2, this was not the case for many of the circuit judges, some of whom had never heard of the 1976 Act. This may in part account for one of the most striking findings of this study, which is the huge variation among judges in handling and deciding on such applications.

One judge, for example, on his first encounter with Section 2, decided to clear the court and hear the application in camera. Later he explained this to the jury as follows:

'I took that course for this reason: I do not know whether it could happen in this case or not, but sometimes in cases the members of the jury have relatives or friends who come to court with them, for perfectly proper reasons, natural interest in what is going on, and they sit in the public gallery. If they heard what went on in the absence of the jury, they might hear something which the judge has decided the jury should not be told. There is another reason as well, quite apart from that reason. If the judge decides that the complainant should not be asked about her previous sexual experience, but it comes out during the hearing in the jury's absence, then it is a little unfair, do you not think, that members of the public who might know this complainant – a neighbour, maybe, who knows about the case and has come along to hear it – should hear all about the complainant's past if it has been private up until that moment.'

It is sad that other judges do not adopt this sensitive and commendable procedure in hearing Section 2 applications. However, the wide variation encountered among judges is potentially far more significant in three further, although related, areas: first, in their commitment to the Act; second, in their decision-making in respect of Section 2; and third, in the extent to which they enforce this part of the law.

Apart from their experience in dealing with this particular section, one factor which affects judges' decisions on these applications is their expressed or implied commitment to the spirit of the Act. Judicial opinions expressed in court on the subject ranged from strong approval to even stronger disapproval, as these extracts illustrate:

Case A: 'Before the 1976 Act, this [cross-examination] was common practice and difficult for a judge to stop. It worked unfairly on the woman: the woman has the right to choose with whom she has sexual intercourse. It does not show that she consented to sexual intercourse with the defendant. The Act intended to stop this illogical unfairness.'

Case B: 'It is not up to me to comment on Parliament, but most of them have no practical experience of how one arrives at the truth in criminal trials.... I think it might be unfair, perhaps even more so in an older woman, to prevent cross-examination on sexual proclivities, but that is what Parliament wants... This wretched section overturns many of our habits in criminal trials.'

How far judges are willing to allow evidence of sexual history to be brought up at the trial is, again, a matter of individual opinion. Although, as mentioned above, the vast majority of applications were at least partly successful, the variation among judges in this area is particularly noteworthy. Although even the most enlightened ones draw the line at excluding evidence of prostitution, it is unquestionable that their decisions in substantially identical cases greatly differ from one another.

As we saw above, the defence sought permission to cross-examine victims in a number of cases about previous complaints of rape they were alleged to have made – sometimes to the police, sometimes just to a friend. It follows, of course, that applications based on these grounds were always based on the implicit assumption that earlier complaints of rape were false allegations. As one judge pertinently pointed out to defence counsel, 'if she had reported it to the police, and there had been a trial and a conviction, you would not be asking to cross-examine on that'.

Evidence of previous rape complaints was excluded in two cases, largely because the judges involved were not willing to endorse the defence assumption that they were unfounded. One of them commented that

'It could only be relevant to show the complainant's tendency to make up a story. There is no evidence that that story was made up. There is nothing in her statement to give grounds for the defence to suggest that it was untrue.'

In two other cases, however, judges took a different view and allowed the cross-examination to go ahead on the grounds that 'The issue is that of previous similar complaints – it would be unfair not to allow it.'

The relevance of previous rape complaints is not the only area where judges differ in their decision-making under Section 2. They also have trouble deciding whether the mere fact of a victim not having been a virgin is the sort of thing juries find helpful in arriving at a verdict. It is interesting to contrast the attitudes of two judges trying factually similar cases where this was an issue.

In both cases, the victim was about 14 years old and according to her statement to the police, had had a very limited degree of sexual experience before the rape incident. The defence on both occasions wanted to cross-examine her about this. One judge allowed it; the other did not. Without clear guidelines, it is not surprising that judges differ so dramatically in their interpretation of the Act. However, lack of uniformity in the implementation of the law clearly presents a problem. This is particularly important and serious if, as we shall see below, evidence of previous sexual experience affects the verdict juries eventually reach.

A quarter of the applications under Section 2 were turned down and the reasons advanced for refusing permission to cross-examine are interesting as they shed some light on the implicit criteria judges use in exercising their discretionary powers in this matter. There is only one type of case where evidence of sexual history is excluded fairly systematically and that is where the defence proposes to probe into a victim's sexual past despite the fact that the defendant has no factual knowledge whatever of this. In one case, for example, two men were accused of raping a young girl they knew by sight. They knew nothing of her previous sexual experience, but the police surgeon's statement (to which the defence has access before the trial) revealed that she had not been a virgin. On that basis, the defence made an application to cross-examine her in very general terms about her sexual background. The judge's reaction was as follows:

'I am not clear about your application. You have no instructions about the complainant's past sexual experience. Thus, you want to embark on a fishing expedition and ask her whether, how, etc. she has had sexual intercourse. Is that right?'

The fact that most defence lawyers are not quite so open about the purpose of their proposed cross-examination poses some difficulty for judges. As one of them candidly remarked, 'I would find this question easier to decide ... if it were to be more of a fishing expedition.' Nevertheless, where applications were turned

84

down, the defence always blatantly proposed to discredit the victim by inquiring into her sexual past in very general terms. But this relationship holds only one way: a proposal of overt mud-slinging seems necessary for the exclusion of such evidence, but it certainly does not guarantee it.

In addition to differences between judges in their commitment to the spirit of the Act and the decisions they reach about admitting sexual history evidence, the variability between them is also apparent with regard to areas where the law, on occasions, is not being applied.

Two judges (including the one so interested in the business of prostitution) systematically questioned the victim about her previous sexual experience without an application from the defence and without any intervention from the prosecution. A similar case was considered by the Court of Appeal, where the following observations were made:

The Judge admitted that he had made a mistake as the argument proceeded. I think I should emphasise that a familiar problem facing the judiciary is that Judges who are immensely experienced in one branch of the law find themselves, apart from their duty, from time to time presiding in other cases, in which their experience may be minimal. That evidently was the situation in this case.[12]

While this may understandably occur in some cases, particularly with a new Act of Parliament, there seems to be no justification for a judge to introduce evidence of previous sexual experience in this way when he is aware of the terms of legislation. In the present study, one judge who made extensive reference to the Act in his summing up explained to the jury that, in his opinion, they ought to have information about the victim's sexual experience. During the trial, after a few questions in cross-examination, he had intervened as follows:

Judge: How old were you at the time of this incident?
Victim: I was sixteen and a half.
Judge: Had you had sex with anyone before this?
Victim: Yes.
Judge: With one boy, or more than one boy?
Victim: More than one.
Judge: At the time, were you going steady with one boy?

85

Victim: Yes.
Judge: So whatever may have been your reputation, were you going steady
and was all that finished with?

On the basis of the present study, it is not possible to estimate the
frequency of this type of judicial intervention in rape trials. This
is nevertheless a disturbing finding insofar as it shows that some
judges are deliberately flouting the intention of Parliament as
embodied in the Act. It is not part of judges' discretion in this
area to give themselves leave, as it were, to cross-examine the
victim and such questioning amounts to a misuse of judicial power.

A second problem area concerns cases where the defence asks
questions of the victim without making an application to the judge
and where such questions relate to some aspect of the victim's
sexual experience. The following are some examples:

Defence counsel: Were you working as a prostitute at the time?
Defence counsel: Had you been to bed with B before? (Referring to a man
named during the trial, other than the defendant)

The extent to which the trial judge intervened in improper cross-
examination of this kind also varied considerably. In some cases,
he sent the jury out as soon as the offending question had been
asked (in this case, inquiring whether the victim had been living
with her boyfriend) and tackled defence counsel about it in fairly
strong terms:

Defence counsel: I apologise. . . .
Judge: That is not enough. You know about that section.
Defence counsel: I'll not suggest that she had any sexual experience. I was
seeking to find out where she was living. I didn't realise the implication
of what I was saying.
Judge: That's outrageous. This was incredibly negligent.

In other cases, and this was far more common, neither the judge
nor the prosecution intervened in any way and the defence were
free to ask a whole series of questions which, on the face of it,
appear to be expressly prohibited by the new Act. In one instance,
the victim was questioned by the defence about her prostitution
in the following way:

'Would you say yours was a risky business? Say in the Piccadilly area, around midnight? It would be a risky business, finding yourself with a strange man in a room? And if a man looks like an Arab, rich and lives in a hotel, that would be OK? In your profession, stealing is very common, isn't it? You are well trained to do that? Isn't that why you had a knife, to help you steal?'

Such questioning was not uncommon in these trials and must also cause some concern with regard to the effectiveness of the law in this area.

All in all, these findings indicate that the practical application of Section 2 of the Sexual Offences (Amendment) Act 1976 is unsatisfactory in a number of respects. It largely incorporates assumptions reflected in earlier case law about the relevance of a victim's previous sexual experience to the issue of consent. Furthermore, the wide variability among judges in their interpretation and application of that section presents a major problem. These difficulties derive largely from the broad way in which legislation was phrased. Clearly, without explicit guidelines, judges must ultimately rely on personal experience and individual perceptions of what constitutes relevance or unfairness, and these are bound to vary. Moreover, in the absence of any criteria, judges are likely to refer to and be guided by the spirit of the old case law in deciding whether a particular piece of evidence is relevant. This probably accounts for the fact that assumptions implicit in those cases are largely reflected in the operation of Section 2.

The problem goes beyond this, however, and is in fact far greater than a discussion of flaws in the applications of Section 2 suggest. First, the Act does nothing to stop the defence from questioning the victim about her previous sexual relationship with the defendant, a position much exploited by the defence. Second, the victim's reputation is often attacked through indirect evidence, implication and suggestion, none of which is covered by the provisions of the new legislation. The next chapter will discuss these problems and their implications in greater detail.

Chapter 6

The importance of being perfect

It takes very little to discredit the victim's sexual reputation. My observation of the court process involved in the trial of rape offences indicates that, even in the absence of solid evidence and valid grounds for an application under Section 2 of the Sexual Offences (Amendment) Act 1976, there is almost invariably some attempt to attack the woman's past sexual behaviour. Defence strategies in this respect fall into two major categories.

The first is to allege that she had previously had consensual intercourse with the defendant, whether or not this is agreed by her. Although the legitimacy of this line of questioning was endorsed by the Heilbron Group, it relies on the rather dubious assumption that once a woman agrees to intercourse with a man, the likelihood is that she will continue to consent at any later stage in their relationship or indeed when the relationship has ended. The rationale here is rather reminiscent of Hale's famous dictum regarding the permanent nature of consent given on marriage.

The second strategy aims to show that the victim is generally 'worldly' or 'experienced'. This relies on the same assumptions as the majority of applications under Section 2, that any sexual experience in a woman indicates indiscriminate consent. Attacks of this sort tend to be used when the defence has no specific or direct knowledge of her sexual experience and they are therefore usually couched in rather vague terms. The use of these defence strategies in the course of trials included in this study will now be discussed in some detail.

The importance of being perfect

Sex with the defendant

If a woman has had a sexual relationship with a man who later attacks and rapes her, no matter how brutally, her rape allegation is likely to be viewed as extremely doubtful. As one defendant graphically exclaimed, after being charged with the rape of his ex-girlfriend: 'You must be fucking mad. How the fuck can I rape a bird if she has two kids of mine?'

Suggestions, let alone solid evidence, that a woman has had sex with the defendant in the past can do a lot to shake her story, and the principle of admitting any evidence relating to that past relationship has long been established. A case in 1827 held that in rape trials, 'the prisoner might show that the prosecutrix had been previously criminally connected with himself'.[1] In 1887, Lord Coleridge summed up the rationale for this decision, still valid today, as follows:

But to reject evidence of her having had connection with the particular person charged with the offence is a wholly different matter, because such evidence is in point as making it so much the more likely that she consented on the occasion charged in the indictment. This line of examination is one which leads directly to the point in issue. Take the case of a woman who has lived, without marriage, for years with the accused before the alleged assault was committed. Can it be reasonably contended that the proof of that fact, or evidence tending to prove that fact, is not material to the issue, and if material to the issue, that such evidence should not be admitted?[2]

In this study, five men based their defence of consent on an allegation of previous sexual acts with the victim. Half of the victims involved denied these allegations. Consider the discrepancy between the defendant and the victim in the following case:

Defendant: Next she came over on a Saturday, a week or so before this. I wasn't surprised because she's been pressing me to take her out and I had no intention of doing it, especially while I was with my wife. She came over after 6pm ... I gave her a Martini .... She'd brought a photo of herself; she gave it to me but I didn't take it. She put a record on. We had sexual intercourse together. We danced, we became friendly.
Victim: He used to say hello to me when he came to the garage. I didn't

know his first name . . . . I had been looking for a room for two or three months, and I had mentioned it to a few customers. [On the day of the rape] another employee at the garage gave me a card with a message written on it, saying 'if you're still interested in a room, come to the following address and ask for the tenant in room 1'. I decided to try this place, and went there about 6pm. Somebody came down, and I said I was looking for the tenant in room 1. I was taken there, and he [the defendant] was there. He introduced himself to me.

What the victim claims is an earlier unreported rape attempt may also be presented as an incident of consensual intercourse:

Defence counsel: Were you quite happy to accept a lift?
Victim: Yes, I've known him a number of years.
Defence counsel: You and he had sex before, didn't you?
Victim: No, but he tried.
Defence counsel: What did you tell the police about this?
Victim: I said that he had tried to have sex with me, but didn't manage to.
Defence counsel: Your statement says there had been an occasion in a ladies' toilet where he tried to kiss you and have sexual intercourse with you, and you didn't let him. Did you tell the police that the defendant succeeded in raping you before?
Victim: No, only that he tried.
Defence counsel: I suggest you've had sexual intercourse with him before, in that toilet, with your consent.
Victim: No.

Where the victim denies defence allegations of prior sexual involvement with the accused, it is not unusual for witnesses to be called to contradict her. In the following case, a friend of the defendant gave this evidence:

'[When I arrived at the flat] the defendant made a sign with his arm which I associated with sex – indicating that he had or was going to have sex with her. Later, he told us that he and the complainant had had sexual intercourse before and that he'd picked her up to give her a lift. When he told me that, I said I'm very surprised, because she looked a very presentable clean young lady. I couldn't believe she lived in a squat and hitched a lift. I said something about her looking like a young virgin. The defendant said, don't you believe it.'

The importance of being perfect

Where the victim agrees that there had been sexual involvement in the past, the defendant is almost invariably acquitted. Cases of this sort afford the defence with an opportunity to present the alleged rape as an overreaction to a domestic dispute which occurred within the framework of an established sexual relationship. It is often suggested that the relationship is closer than the victim is willing to admit or, in some cases, that it amounts to cohabitation. In any event, she is likely to be cross-examined in considerable detail about practically all aspects of the relationship, however irrelevant they are to the trial:

Defence counsel: How would you describe your relationship with the defendant?
Victim: I was going out with him, but it wasn't a permanent relationship. Sometimes he didn't use to come round at all .... He stayed the night, but not most nights. Just some nights.
Defence counsel: It's important for you that nobody should think that he lived at your flat because of social security payments, isn't it?
Victim: Yes ...
Defence counsel: I suggest he lived there, that this was his home all the time.
Victim: No.

Where the relationship between the victim and the defendant was no longer a sexual one by the time of the alleged rape, the picture of their past relationship is sometimes compounded by suggestions of promiscuity on the part of the woman. This may be couched in rather general terms, as in the following example:

Defendant: I had been living with the complainant for over a year. We'd been having arguments. I left because there were too many men. She has so many men, you couldn't keep count. She'd have anyone.

Another strategy in this type of case is to normalise the alleged rape in the light of the nature of the relationship between the victim and the defendant. The following example speaks for itself; it is taken from a case where the victim and defendant had in the past lived together and both agreed that their relationship had ended some months before the rape incident:

Defence counsel: I suggest that sex with the defendant was, previously, quite a stormy affair.

Victim: Yes.

Defence counsel: Physical violence was used from time to time, by the defendant to you.

Victim: Yes.

. . .

Defence counsel: You didn't mind some roughness, some beating up?

Victim: Yes – he hadn't beaten me up during sex. He had beaten me before sex on previous occasions. He used to beat me up too, irrespective of sex. Sometimes, he was gentle.

Defence counsel: No beating stopped you having sex with him later, that was the pattern of life with him?

Victim: Yes.

Defence counsel: And you didn't mind?

Victim: They weren't severe beatings. He was very demanding. If I refused sex, he'd threaten. It was only like that towards the latter part of the relationship.

Defence counsel: That night [rape] was no different to others – the beating may have been more severe, but that's all.

Victim: It was very different. If I didn't want to give in before, he'd beat me for it. Only very occasionally would the beatings end up in sexual intercourse.

Defence counsel: I suggest that on that day, the only abnormality was that there were two women. Otherwise, the violence and the oral sex had both happened before.

Victim: It was very different.

Defence counsel: Only in the degree of violence.

Victim: Yes, and all the other bits and pieces.

Defence counsel: There had been other occasions when you had consented

. . . .

Victim: If I had consented in the first place, I'd never have got beaten up.

The defendant in this case was acquitted. He was, however, subsequently sentenced to life imprisonment for the rape of a woman who had not been as severely injured as his ex-girlfriend, but who had had no previous sexual contact with him.

The existence of a prior sexual relationship serves not only to discredit complaints of rape, but also to provide a wealth of possible motives for false allegations. These are often very convincing to a jury insofar as they make sense in terms of the general folklore of rape and notions of female sexuality and psychology. The suggestion that women claim rape in order to avoid responsibility, for example, is a common one:

The importance of being perfect

Defence counsel: I suggest you wanted to blame somebody for getting you pregnant, so that you could justify your pregnancy to your relatives.

The defence may also claim that the rape complaint was made for financial gain. In one instance, defence counsel opened his case as follows:

'The defendant provided well for this girl and treated the place as his home. He was of course distressed to be locked out, away from his goods and his girl. If the whole case is about that girl exploiting that distress and exaggerating it, so that she can hold on to the possessions that she on social security couldn't afford – that has to be taken into account in considering the rape and common assault counts.'

The most commonly attributed motive for rape allegations in such cases is spite. This relies on Congreve's poetic notion that 'Heav'n has no rage, like love to hatred turn'd, Nor Hell a fury, like a woman scorn'd', a line which was quoted during the parliamentary debates of the Sexual Offences (Amendment) Bill, as well as (usually inaccurately) during the trials included in this study. Here is how some defendants elaborate on the idea in court:

'I woke up to being slapped around the face. I just hit out, slapped her back. She kept asking if I loved her, and I said I still loved my wife. There was a row about it. She said was going to get me for this.'

'It was at her invitation and with her consent that we had sexual intercourse. After, she asked if I still wanted to go back to my wife. I said I couldn't just decide. I said I couldn't just ignore my wife and I could only be friends with her [the complainant]. She was upset by that – I told her to be reasonable. Then she went to the loo. I thought she was coming back, but that was the last I saw of her.'

Sanders has argued that rape law operates on the assumption that a woman's worth is measured in terms of her decision to have sex with a man: 'if she does so voluntarily on one occasion, her worth is less on another if the man rapes her'.[3] Although the numbers involving such relationships in this study are small, the outcome of these cases lends support to the above assertion. With one exception, all the men who had had a previous sexual relationship with the woman involved were acquitted. The only conviction was in a somewhat unusual case, where the defendant and the victim had had sexual intercourse on one occasion several years before the rape but had not seen one another at all in the intervening period, until he broke into her flat, forcibly disconnected the telephone, threatened her with a knife and left the following day, having written a note apologizing for what he had done.

The beauty of innuendoes

It has been noted that Western society tends to adopt a split view towards women: Holmstrom and Burgess have termed this the 'Madonna-Whore complex'.[4] The roots of this are to be found in Victorian sexual morality which made a clear distinction between 'good' and 'bad' women. The sexual ideology which prevailed at the time when much of the case law relating to sexual history evidence was developing has been extensively documented by contemporary sociologists and historians, who have shown basic agreement about its main features:

the polarisation of women into the chaste and the depraved, the virgin and the whore; the virginity ethic, manifested alike in the fierceness with which 'innocence' was protected in young and adult woman, and the 'defloration mania' which dominated English brothels in the 1880s . . . .[5]

Although such a view bears no resemblance to the sexual practices of women today, the double standard remains and provides the basis of what is frequently a highly successful line of defence in rape cases. The legal system epitomises double standards by effectively punishing women and girls for behaviour not only overlooked but actually admired and encouraged in men and boys. Insofar as a sexually active woman will be seen as a 'bad' woman, and therefore an unlikely rape victim, it becomes important for the defence in the trial to portray her as such. Depending on the nature and circumstances of the case, this may be done in a variety of ways. Where the prosecution allege that the victim had been a virgin prior to the rape, the defence may challenge this and attempt to present her as sexually experienced:

Victim: I was a virgin. I had tried to have sexual intercourse but couldn't.
Defence counsel: Did your boyfriend never try to penetrate you?

Victim: I don't know really ... we didn't go all the way ... nothing really happened. After that, I went to see a doctor and had an internal examination.

Defence counsel: [On the occasion of the alleged rape] you say two people raped you?

Victim: Yes.

Defence counsel: Was there any bleeding?

Victim: No.

Defence counsel: There were swabs taken from you and there was no sign of blood from loss of virginity. Do you still say you were a virgin?

Victim: Yes.

Defence counsel: How is that possible, without any blood? It's impossible. I suggest you are lying, you'd had sex before.

It may also be implied that the victim's familiarity with sexual terms or expressions is indicative of experience on her part. A 15-year-old victim, whose virginity had already been disputed at some length by the defence, was cross-examined as follows:

Defence counsel: How did you know Frank [the first defendant] was coming if you've never had sex with him before?

Victim: I knew from people talking ... mum and the police helped me.

Defence counsel: Did he ejaculate?

Victim: (Made no reply)

Defence counsel: Did you feel any wet?

Victim: No.

Defence counsel: Had you used any contraceptive?

Victim: No.

Defence counsel: Did you know Tom [the second defendant] was coming?

Victim: I knew with Frank becaused he shouted it out to Tom.

Defence counsel: But you've said that you noticed Frank coming in some other way. It was Tom who shouted out.

Victim: I don't remember which – one of them did.

Another technique is to question about any contraceptive used and to base suggestions of promiscuity on her answers. In the following example, this is compounded by the implied existence of a boyfriend, although there was no evidence at the trial that he did in fact exist:

Defence counsel: Did you use any contraceptive?

Victim: I was on the pill.

Defence counsel: Did you say to him [the defendant] that you had a regular
    boyfriend who was away?
Victim: Yes.
Defence counsel: And that meanwhile, you went out with someone else?
Victim: No.
Defence counsel: Wasn't it this second boyfriend who did not turn up that
    day?
Victim: No, that was my boyfriend. I later found out that he was away.
Judge: What is the relevance of this?
Defence counsel: My client felt that this woman was used to having casual
    relations with men.

The presence of vaginal infections may be used to imply sexual
experience and promiscuity, even where there is medical evidence
that such infections were not transmitted through sexual contact.
The existence of some such infection is occasionally suggested by
the defence without any independent evidence at all:

Defendant: Yeah, I had sex with her, but not completely. I thought I
    might catch something off her, it turned me off.

Even in the absence of direct questions in cross-examination about
vaginal infections, the defence may capitalise on the fact that these
have connotations of being 'dirty' and 'unclean'. One woman
suffering from non-specific urethritis was cross-examined as follows:

Defence counsel: I suggest you were dressed in a slovenly fashion, with a
    hole in your dress.
Victim: No, I was a manageress in a boutique ...
Defence counsel: Were you managing to keep yourself clean and tidy at
    that period of time?
Victim: Yes.
Defence counsel: The defendant also says that you were slovenly that
    evening.
Victim: No.
Defence counsel: When he first saw you at the pub, you looked slovenly
    to him.
Victim: No, I had a new dress on.

Later in that case, at the request of another defence counsel, the
judge went on to probe the victim even further about her habits
of personal cleanliness:

The importance of being perfect

Judge: I want to ask you a personal question. There was some semen found inside you, and I want to clarify the question asked from you about sexual intercourse. Have you a bath at home?

Victim: Yes.

Judge: How often a week do you have a bath?

Victim: Two to three times.

Judge: This took place on June 28th. How long before did you have a bath?

Victim: Probably the night before.

Judge: Certainly not two to three nights before?

Victim: I think it was the night before.

Defence counsel may try to show similarities between features of the alleged rape and aspects of the victim's everyday life in an attempt to normalise the former. The following example is an extract from a trial where three black youths were charged with the rape of two white girls. Here, the suggestion was that the circumstances surrounding the alleged offence were not very different from the girls' everyday activities:

Defence counsel: Did you often have boys there [at the flat] until 3am?

Victim: No.

Defence counsel: Did boys used to come round at night?

Victim: In the evening, yes.

Defence counsel: Had the boys coming to the flat nearly always been black?

Victim: Not all of them, some.

Defence counsel: The question was, apart from the girl, were they nearly all black?

Victim: No.

Defence counsel: Do you know what a blues party is? Soul music, low lights?

Victim: Yes.

In some cases suggestions of sexual experience are made almost in passing and there is no attempt to relate this directly to the issues in the trial. For example, one woman was asked about her divorce which preceded the alleged rape by some eight months:

Defence counsel: On what grounds was your husband divorcing you?

Victim: Desertion. He also tried to put in adultery, but that wasn't true. He also tried to say I was mentally disturbed.

Such apparently casual questions and the replies they elicit never-theless serve to discredit the victim and to portray her as sexually 'easy'. Even when she is not cross-examined in this way, the defendant's evidence may serve the same purpose:

Defendant: She seemed very liberated and attractive. She was thumbing a lift, anyway .... She told me about her own private life, that she was sick of her boyfriend who slept around too much. She told me she was intending to sleep around too. I think she mentioned that later. She said she'd slept with her boyfriend's best friend, to spite him.

On other occasions, there is nothing subtle or casual about attacks on the victim's sexual reputation. The following example is an extract from the particularly vicious cross-examination of a woman who had been allegedly raped and severely beaten by four men, all of whom were total strangers to her:

Defence counsel: I suggest you started to flirt with other men in the pub, to show how little you cared for your boyfriend.
Victim: No.
Defence counsel: Were you in the habit of going to pubs by yourself, in the evening?
Victim: No, it was the first time. I went there in a temper, to get away from my parents and my boyfriend.
Defence counsel: I suggest you did, and that is why you walked out of the pub with the first young man who came along.
Victim: No, I didn't.
Defence counsel: Why talk to your boyfriend in the pub about your first husband using a milk bottle inside you?
Victim: I was hoping he'd get embarrassed and leave. I'd lost control, I was near to tears.
Defence counsel: At that stage, I suggest, other people joined in the conversation and someone said, 'who's got a bottle then'. You shared the joke, showing what kind of a person you really were, prepared to have sex with strangers.
Victim: No.
Defence counsel: You were drawing attention to the bottle in a way that you'd enjoyed it, that you wanted it repeated. Isn't that right?
Victim: No.

Evidence from the various defendants in the trial, partly perhaps because of the impact of repetition, reinforced the image that counsel had tried to create in cross-examination:

The importance of being perfect

First defendant: A girl came in [the pub] and she had a row with her bloke. She was buying drinks. She was putting herself about, just a slag. It was 'hello, darling, you in the red shirt, I fancy you'.

Second defendant: She was drunk when she came in. She got herself a gin. She was joined by her boyfriend and bought a pint. She was over everybody. She smelt like an old fishpond. She pulled someone to her knee, she was dancing about.

Third defendant: The way she behaved, I thought she was a bit of an old bag.

The fourth defendant pleaded guilty and told the court how he and his friends dragged the victim into a park and took turns at raping her while the others held her down and hit her to stop her from screaming. He was the only one to go to prison for the offence: the others were acquitted.

The above extracts illustrate ways in which women's sexual reputation is discredited in court. It is, however, difficult to convey in print the hostile, contemptuous and insinuating tone in which the pertinent questions are often asked. In one trial, for example, the alleged victim was questioned as follows:

Defence counsel: Do girls in your flat often get raped?
Victim: No ...
Defence counsel: Do they rape easily?

Similarly, facial expressions of utter incredulity often accompany questions such as this:

Victim: I had sex with him because it was done by force – I had no choice.
Judge: How much did you get paid for it?

In this chapter, I have tried to show that the defence can and does use a number of strategies to discredit sexually the alleged victim of rape and that this may be done with considerable success outside the scope of Section 2 of the Sexual Offences (Amendment) Act 1976. Indirect evidence and suggestion are brought into play and the introduction of new legislation has not, and cannot in isolation, influence this aspect of court practice. The importance of information and speculation thus introduced is invariably stressed in defence counsel's closing speech:

'The girls themselves are worth looking at. One of the complainants' hymen was ruptured before this incident. You might find it shocking that she was prepared to bed down in the same room as any man.'

What is perhaps more surprising is that the prosecution also tends to acknowledge the relevance of evidence introduced in this way. Indeed, they may go so far as actively to draw the jury's attention to these aspects of the defence case:

Prosecution counsel: You have heard evidence about the sort of girl she is – you have to take that into account as a background of the case.

And juries are certainly given plenty of background on the victim before retiring to consider their verdict. In this study, evidence relating to the sexual past of 96 per cent of the victims was introduced in some way in the trial. For 20 per cent, the prosecution brought in evidence of virginity; for 17 per cent, there was an allegation of previous sexual intercourse with the defendant; and for 59 per cent, evidence was brought in of prior sexual experience with someone else. How far do juries take the woman's sexual history into account in arriving at their verdict?

The outcome of a criminal trial is dependent on a number of extra-legal factors, including the judge's conduct of the proceedings, the lawyers involved, the impression created by witnesses on both sides, as well as the nature and presentation of the evidence. Another major factor is the jury, whose role and impact in this respect have been the subject of much controversy as well as some academic study.

Research in this field has been hampered by the secrecy that continues to surround the jury's deliberations. Nevertheless, there seems to be general agreement among supporters and opponents of the jury system that the jury, more or less consciously, brings its own values and interpretations to bear on any case. With particular reference to rape, Kalven and Zeisel's classic American jury study argues that the jury goes beyond determining consent:

it goes on to weigh the woman's conduct in the prior history of the affair. It closely, and often harshly, scrutinizes the female complainant and is moved to be lenient with the defendant whenever there are suggestions of contributory behaviour on her part.[6]

The question now arises as to whether evidence of her sexual past has any bearing on decision-making in court. Is having this investigated in court merely distressing and unpleasant for the victim or does it actually help to persuade the jury of the defendant's innocence?

There is a staggering difference in the conviction rates of those defendants whose victims were virgins, or of whose sexual past the jury knew nothing, and those accused of raping women known to have had prior sexual experience. This highlights the perceived importance of chastity in the 'genuine' victim of rape: virginity all but guarantees a conviction. In this sample, only one out of a total of seventeen defendants was acquitted of the rape of a virgin or a woman whose sexual past was not referred to during the trial. That is a conviction rate of 94 per cent.

At the other end of the spectrum, the conviction rate among those accused of raping a woman whose sexual reputation was markedly discredited during the trial was 48 per cent. This includes women who had in the past suffered from sexually transmitted diseases, those who had a reputation in the local community for being sexually available, those who had been involved in sexual intercourse with a number of persons within a short period of time and those who were alleged to be prostitutes. It is also interesting to point out that nearly all those defendants who were acquitted on the judge's direction, i.e. whose fate was not felt to be safe with the jury, were accused of raping women alleged to have such sexual histories.

It is unquestionable that the counterdenunciation of the victim, particularly as far as her sexual reputation is concerned, is a prominent feature of rape trials and an important determinant of the verdict. However, her sexuality is not the only thing that can be counted against her: the next chapter considers how far other aspects of her behaviour and attributes become the focus of attention and the extent to which these are also linked to the outcome of the trial.

Chapter 7

The prime suspect

———————◆———————

One factor which caused considerable concern to the Heilbron Group was that in a rape trial, the victim is often as much on trial as the defendant. We have seen how this comes about with respect to her sexual history – but is she also 'on trial' in any other sense? This chapter discusses how far her non-sexual attributes and her behaviour around the time of the rape are scrutinised in court. Specific aspects of her behaviour considered here are perceived provocation, active resistance to the defendant and promptness in reporting the matter to the police. The chapter will also examine the relationship between these factors and the jury's verdict.

Is she a 'nice girl'?

We have seen that the victim's chastity and sexual reputation remain crucial issues in rape trials. Her general character, however, also seems to be a salient factor and attempts are frequently made to discredit her in this respect. Anything other than totally 'proper' and 'respectable' behaviour may be used for this purpose. The following are examples of some defence questions aiming at this general area:

'Are you living on social security?'
'Did you tell the defendant that you were in a poor financial situation?'
'Where did you meet the defendant?' (eliciting the reply that it was in a probation hostel)
'Did your mother know that you were staying at the party all night?'
'Had you lived in squats before?'
'Did you know that your boyfriend had had trouble with the police over drugs?'

The most common strategies used to discredit the victim's character are to bring out information or make allegations about her alcohol and drug use, her criminal record and her psychiatric history.

The defence may go to great lengths to establish how much the victim had had to drink, particularly when she denies heavy consumption. One victim, who said that she had half a pint of beer to drink on the day of the rape, had her blood alcohol level checked and the scientific officer in charge of the analysis was cross-examined as follows:

Witness: It's not possible that only half a pint of beer was consumed five hours earlier. That would have dissipated in five hours.
Defence counsel: Would excitement make the alcohol dissipate slower?
Witness: No, I have allowed for that. There had to be more alcohol taken at that time .... I would expect about four and a half measures of spirits, or four or five half pints to have been drunk five hours earlier.
Judge: What about the previous night's drinks? If she had five double Bacardis between midnight and 5am?
Witness: That could still produce that amount of blood alcohol after five hours. It might well affect the reading.
Defence counsel: But if she had no drinks after 5.30am, would that still have an effect fourteen hours later?
Witness: It's just possible, yes.
Defence counsel: Up to that level?
Witness: I'd make it a bit less.

Such evidence is often linked to the issue of consent: in particular, the presence of alcohol and/or drugs may be used to imply that the victim must have agreed to sex with the defendant:

Defence counsel: [Around that time] were you drinking heavily?
Victim: Yes. I was under the doctor.
Defence counsel: Is it right that in August you were fined for being drunk and disorderly?
Victim: Yes.
Defence counsel: Isn't it right that you were very drunk in the car on the way to the party, as you said in your statement?
Victim: I wasn't feeling drunk.
Defence counsel: Haven't you been in pubs enough to see people when they have had too much to drink? I suggest that everything that happened at the flat was because you had had too much to drink.

Alternatively, it may be suggested that the victim's alcohol intake and/or drug consumption so affected her memory of the events that her evidence must be considered unreliable. In the following example, the victim was on a course of Librium, but denied taking any on the day of the rape incident. The defence, nevertheless, continued to operate on the assumption that she had mixed alcohol and this drug and cross-examined the doctor in the case as to the probable effects of this combination:

Witness: Persons taking Librium and alcohol together may appear more drunk than they in fact are. It makes them feel more abandoned and outgoing .... They would be unsteady, more likely to bump into things. If Librium had been taken with alcohol, that could affect the reliability of the girl's account – as much as in someone who is just drunk.

A victim with a criminal record is a real bonus for the defence. In such cases, she is almost invariably subjected to lengthy cross-examination about her convictions. One young girl with an extremely disturbed childhood spent largely in local authority care (probably as a result of sexual assaults committed on her by her father from the age of 8 upwards) was, in cross-examination, taken through each of her numerous encounters with the police in some detail. The suggestion was then made that these provided her with a strong motive to go through with her rape allegation:

Defence counsel: I suggest you thought that if you withdrew your allegations, you'd be in serious trouble.
Victim: I knew I'd be in trouble.
Defence counsel: Have you been interviewed [by the police] about other offences, like clipping?
Victim: Yes – that means getting men's money and running off. You make out you'll do business with them.
Defence counsel: You admitted doing this last September for some weeks. Were you earning £100 to £200 pounds a week, doing this?
Victim: Yes.
Defence counsel: Were you charged?
Victim: Yes, but it got dropped.
Defence counsel: Did that have anything to do with your giving evidence here?
Victim: I don't know, I can't remember.

Defence counsel: Were you told why the charges were dropped?
Victim: I don't know.

More commonly, however, evidence that the victim has a criminal record is simply used to cast doubt on her overall credibility. As one defence counsel argued, 'I want to put to her her conviction for shoplifting – this shows her dishonesty, her unreliability.'

One of the main rape myths, as we have already discussed, is that women have a marked tendency to make hysterical, unfounded allegations of rape for a variety of somewhat obscure psychological reasons. Where these hidden motives can be linked to an actual history of psychiatric disorder, this affords confirmation of the victim's lack of stability, reliability and, consequently, credibility. Cross-examination as to her psychiatric history may take the form of what has been termed a 'fishing expedition', prompted, for example, by her spontaneous mention of feeling depressed:

Defence counsel: When you met the two girls, do you remember if you told them you'd just come out of hospital?
Victim: No, I might have said that I worked in a hospital.
Defence counsel: Have you ever been to a mental hospital?
Victim: No.
Defence counsel: Or received psychiatric treatment?
Victim: No.

However, when the defence have something more tangible and concrete to hand, such as evidence of suicide attempts, periods of hospitalisation in psychiatric institutions or outpatient psychiatric treatment, no matter how long before the rape incident, these are certain to be explored in great detail during the trial:

Defence counsel: [About two years ago] you were in a hospital for five months, were you not? A mental hospital?
Victim: Yes. I was there because I cut my wrists.
Defence counsel: In an attempt to kill yourself?
Victim: I don't know . . . .
Defence counsel: How old were you at the time?
Victim: 16
Defence counsel: That wasn't the only time you cut your wrists. There were many other times, were there not?

The prime suspect

That the introduction of this sort of information is intended to discredit the victim is unquestionable. As if the importance of the unspoken links between psychiatric history, lack of stability and false allegations of rape were not obvious, these are made explicit for the jury in defence speeches:

Defence counsel: Allegations of a sexual nature, members of the jury, are so easy to bring and so hard to refute .... We have here a girl of 18. We know from the scars on her wrists that there is some history of attempted suicide. She might be confusing this [rape] with another incident.

There are occasions when several or all of these factors are said to be present in the same victim, as in the case of a young woman in her mid-twenties, recently separated from her husband and the mother of a small child. There was a custody dispute between her and her husband and, at the time of the rape incident, her child was in local authority care. After the separation, she was feeling very depressed, began to drink more than usual and went to her doctor about this. She was sent for outpatient treatment for her depression and drink problem and was seeing a psychiatrist, once a fortnight for about three months, when she began to feel better. During this time, she persistently turned up late for work and eventually lost her job. She was closely questioned about all these matters by defence counsel who suggested that she was mentally unstable, clearly disturbed with a grudge against men and an unfit mother with a serious drinking problem whose evidence could not be relied on.

Such efforts at discrediting a victim's evidence appear to be highly successful. If she is shown to be blameworthy in one area, she will be presented as blameworthy altogether and cannot hope to aspire to the status of the innocent, genuine victim that the stereotype favours. Fifty-two per cent of those defendants whose victims had been markedly discredited[1] during the trial were convicted, as compared to 77 per cent of the rest. The difference is statistically significant, i.e. not due to chance factors alone and supports the view that women who are seen as 'respectable' have a better chance of substantiating their rape complaint than those depicted in a less favourable light.

Before the rape

The victim's sexual history and her character are both factors totally independent of the rape. Not surprisingly, however, she is even more likely to be criticised for her behaviour before, during and after the rape incident.

When dealing with the circumstances leading up to the rape, defence efforts are focused on demonstrating that she provoked the assault and that the assault, if indeed it took place at all, was her fault. Attempts to show victim precipitation, as it is sometimes called, range from comments about her clothes and appearance to suggestions of sexually provocative language, gestures or behaviour towards the defendant. The approaches used at this stage confirm the continuing importance of the old stereotype that rape happens because of uncontrollable urges aroused by sexually provocative women.

A common defence technique is to comment on the victim's clothes and appearance. Although society expects women to look attractive, if they happen to become rape victims, this may be used against them. The implication is that their appearance is indicative of their sexual mores and behaviour. In his closing speech, one defence counsel described the victim in these terms:

'A girl wearing hippy sort of clothes, tight jeans and plimsolls, walking around alone late at night, getting into a car with three men, having just left the flat of a fourth man .... '

Another victim, whose assailant broke in while she was asleep, was cross-examined as to what she usually wore in bed:

Defence counsel: You wore no clothes in bed?
Victim: No. I had a quilt on and a sheet. I was sitting up in bed.
Defence counsel: Were your breasts showing?
Victim: No.
Defence counsel: I suggest that the quilt slipped and your breasts were showing.

Another frequent defence strategy is to suggest that the victim did not object to being in the company of the defendant and/or in the situation where the rape occurred. This is then construed as

implied consent to sexual intercourse as well. The following example is taken from a case where the victim, who knew the defendant,
accepted a lift home from him. Her cross-examination went as
follows:

Defence counsel: You got off the bike before him or he wouldn't have been
    able to get off.
Victim: No, he got off first. He kind of pulled me off.
Defence counsel: Did you resent that?
Victim: No.
Defence counsel: So he helped you off.
Victim: Same difference.
Defence counsel: Were you willing to get off?
Victim: Yes.

At this stage, the judge intervened:

Judge: On the bench, you expected a bit of necking, didn't you?
Victim: No.
Judge: Why on earth did you think you were sitting on the bench?
Victim: He said to talk.
Judge: (looking at the jury, incredulous) I see . . .

If it can be shown beyond doubt that she accompanied him
willingly or that she allowed him into her home, her behaviour
becomes even more suspicious. As one defence counsel told the
jury:

'She went into the car and to the flat willingly – you must consider
this in deciding whether sexual intercourse with [him] was without her
consent. Consider her getting into the car – is that a risk any ordinary
person would take? In the light of her admission of him taking her hand,
and her going along anyway, her behaviour was not inconsistent with
consent to sexual intercourse.'

This followed cross-examination aiming to establish how the victim
came to be in the company of the defendants. The existence of a
prior relationship between them (he was a friend of her sister's
and known to her for many years) was in this case underplayed by
the defence, for good reason: it emerged that at one time she used

to visit him regularly in prison. At the trial, she was questioned at length about her reasons for going to his flat willingly:

Defence counsel: Would you have gone for a drink with the defendant?
Victim: Yes.
Defence counsel: If the other man got into the car, why didn't you leave?
Victim: I thought I was safe with the defendant. It didn't cross my mind that something like this would happen.
Defence counsel: But you were prepared to go shopping with them, and to the defendant's flat?
Victim: Yes. I knew the defendant. I trusted him.

In other cases, it may be suggested that the victim actively sought the company of the defendant and was the one to initiate contact with him. This is then used to imply that she was 'asking for' what happened, as the following extract illustrates:

Defence counsel: You told [your friend] to fuck off because you wanted to stay at the pub.
Victim: No.
Defence counsel: Having said that, you joined the coloured men [the defendants] and asked one of them what he was doing after the pub.
Victim: No.
Defence counsel: He told you he was going to a club.
Victim: No.
Defence counsel: When he told you he was going to a club, you asked if you could go with him because you liked reggae music.
Victim: No.
Defence counsel: It had been suggested that you should go back to his place to listen to music,
Victim: No ... .
Defence counsel: and you were happy to go there?
Victim: Not at first. There was nothing said about a club.

Defence counsel for the other defendant at this trial went on to question her as follows:

Defence counsel: I suggest you made it quite clear that you wanted to be with these men, rather than with your friend, even earlier when he was still at the pub. You said he could fuck off, you wanted to have a good time.
Victim: No. ...

Defence counsel: You wanted some kicks. Why did you agree to go to a party and then creep out?
Victim: No, I meant later on, when I saw no one there – that's when I wanted to creep out.

The defence may imply that the victim was 'out to have a good time' in general terms and was actively looking for a pick-up, or at least gave the appearance of being available. The following extract is taken from a case where the victim had spent the evening preceding the rape in a disco with a girlfriend:

Defence counsel: You didn't go with your boyfriend, so you just danced with anybody and everybody?
Victim: No, just people we knew.
Defence counsel: I suggest you danced many times with the defendant.
Victim: No.

Occasionally, the victim is portrayed as not just sexually available, but as engaging in behaviour which is explicitly sexual and provocative; the obvious implication here is that such behaviour is indicative not just of consent, but of active participation too:

Defence counsel: I suggest that you put a record on and started to dance around on your own. While you were doing that, the defendants sat down and opened three bottles of lager.
Victim: I put no music on and didn't dance.
Defence counsel: You were offered a lager with a glass – you just took the bottle. You continued dancing and drank it rather quickly.
Victim: No.
Defence counsel: You went on dancing and went up to one of the defendants and told him to get up and dance.
Victim: This is all being made up.
Defence counsel: He said he wasn't dancing. You grabbed him by the arm and pulled him to his feet. ... You said you were a bad woman and ripped open your blouse. That's when the various buttons fell off.
Victim: It's all lies.
Defence counsel: [Later] you told one of the defendants that you liked him and asked where the bedroom was.
Victim: It's all lies.
Defence counsel: I suggest you said you were tired and wanted to relax.

The suggestion is sometimes made that consensual intimacy of some sort took place between the defendant and the victim immediately before the rape incident, which is another way of implying that consent to intercourse can hardly be a realistic issue:

Defence counsel: I suggest you were enjoying yourself [at the party], away from your boyfriend.
Victim: That's not true.
Defence counsel: You danced with the defendant?
Victim: I've never seen him before.
Defence counsel: I suggest you flirted with him, holding him tight as you danced.

A defence witness reinforced this picture by describing the victim's behaviour as follows:

'She came in alone, and stood in the hall looking around. I danced with her, a very, very, close dance like young people do today. I danced with her to half a dozen tunes or more. She was close all the time. I thought her attitude very rude. ... Later, she danced with another bloke [the defendant] for about two records. She was the same, very close to him. They were talking, I saw them. They seemed familiar.'

Occasionally, a somewhat greater degree of consensual intimacy is suggested:

Defence counsel: I suggest you danced many times with the defendant.
Victim: No.
Defence counsel: And while dancing with him, you allowed him to kiss you?
Victim: Not that I remember.
Defence counsel: I suggest he danced with you on a number of occasions and you allowed him to kiss you.

Defence counsel invariably engages in rather detailed cross-examination in cases where the victim agrees that some quasi-sexual contact occurred between her and the defendant before the rape. This is then presented as consent to preliminary sexual activities and taken to imply consent to full intercourse:

Defence counsel: You were quite happy to go and sit with him on the balcony?
Victim: Yes.
Defence counsel: There, you talked and kissed, you say?

Victim: Yes.
Defence counsel: Kissing with some enthusiasm?
Victim: Yes.
Defence counsel: There are several kinds of kisses – were you French kissing?
Victim: We might have been.
Defence counsel: And you were quite happy and content for that to happen?
Victim: Yes.
Defence counsel: And was it suggested in the conversation that he walk you to the bus?
Victim: Yes, we both decided that.
Defence counsel: And you were perfectly happy for him to do that?
Victim: Yes.
Defence counsel: [On the way to the bus stop] he asked you for a goodnight kiss, and you were quite happy for him to do that, were you not?
Victim: Yes.
Defence counsel: He had his arms around you, pressed against you and you against him, isn't that right?
Victim: I think he did have his arm around me, in a sort of embrace.

The assumption here seems to be that a woman who flirts with a man, or kisses him but then retracts from intercourse, has so much responsibility for the offence herself that this negates the occurrence of it altogether. In this particular case, prosecution counsel overtly condoned and indeed supported the logic of acquitting in his closing speech:

Prosecution counsel: If she really said 'yes' up to the last minute and then changed her mind, you might think that she asked for it.

On occasions, the judge may try to redress the balance by pointing out to the jury the dangers of inferring consent to intercourse from such behaviour, as the following extract illustrates:

Judge: It's true that the girls put themselves in that situation. It would have been wiser to run out, or shout. On the other hand, put yourselves in that situation. Don't say they were silly to be there in the first place – that has nothing to do with it at all.

Holmstrom and Burgess's American study which has been referred to above found that the majority of convictions involved cases where the victim was unwilling to accompany the assailant to wherever the offence took place. In this study, the victim's consent to being in the situation[2] does not, in itself, correlate with the verdict. This may be a function of the small numbers involved; however, when the overall effect of all the factors favouring conviction are considered, consent to being in the defendant's company in conjunction with other factors may well tip the scales.

... during

Next, the victim's behaviour at the very time of the rape comes under scrutiny and this usually raises the issue of just how much she resisted.

The Heilbron Group's report emphasised the element of consent in rape and argued that the use of force and violence should not be regarded as an essential ingredient of it:

It is ... wrong to assume that the woman must show signs of injury or that she must always physically resist before there can be a conviction for rape. We have found this erroneous assumption held by some and therefore hope that our recommendations will go some way to dispel it.[3]

Consequently, the definition of rape contained in the 1976 Act makes no reference to the need to establish physical resistance.

Nevertheless, an observation of court procedure clearly shows that violence over and above the rape is still deemed to be necessary for a conviction. If the woman can show that she physically resisted her attacker and sustained injuries in the process, she is much more likely to substantiate her allegation of rape than if she only offered verbal or passive resistance. As defence counsel commented in one such case,

'The rapes one reads about in the press are savage ones, where consent does not arise. That's a straightforward case of rape, where the issues are clear. There has been a tragic misunderstanding here.'

The need to look for signs of injury is frequently underlined for the jury who are told that in 'real' rape cases one should always expect to find evidence of physical violence. The following extracts illustrate this point:

Defence counsel: There is no medical evidence, only an old bruise. There is no scientific evidence – in cases such as this, one is accustomed to buttons missing, fingernail scratches, torn clothes. There is nothing like that here.

Judge: Regarding the evidence of the girl, I have come to the conclusion that none of the things happened that one might expect: no scratches, no pain, no injuries, no evidence that she struggled.

There is a great deal of conflicting opinion, incidentally, as to whether or not it is wise for a woman to resist her attacker physically. Lack of resistance will certainly look bad in court, while fighting back may expose the victim to further physical injuries. Groth and Cohen confirm the unpredictability of the effect of resistance on the attacker from first-hand interviews with convicted rapists, who were asked about their reaction to it: 'One rapist answered, "When my victim screamed, I ran"; another said, "When my victim screamed, I cut her throat" '.[4]

Whatever the risks to herself, physical resistance is expected of the 'genuine' victim. In cross-examination, defence counsel usually makes a point of establishing just exactly how active her resistance to the accused had been. The standard strategy is to try to show that she did not put up a very convincing struggle and that she missed many opportunities of escape. In the absence of any evidence of marked physical injury, the victim's cross-examination may be centred entirely around this issue:

Defence counsel: I suggest you made a weak attempt at moving his hand and when he persisted, you stopped objecting.
Victim: No.
Defence counsel: I suggest he didn't do anything to force you – he didn't put his hand over your mouth.
Victim: Yes he did and he had his hands behind my back.
Defence counsel: Did you scratch his face?
Victim: You don't think of that at the time.
Defence counsel: Surely, it's instinctive?
Victim: I didn't have the strength to do anything.
Defence counsel: Did you try and run away?
Victim: Yes.
Defence counsel: Did you hit him?
Victim: No.
Defence counsel: Did you push him away?

Victim: Yes.
Defence counsel: Kick him?
Victim: You don't think of things like, I've already explained.
Defence counsel: Did you do any of those things?
Victim: I was too scared.

Having sustained injuries in the course of the rape is not necessarily enough to convince a jury of lack of consent. The defence may suggest that the particular woman's injuries are not as serious as they would have been in a 'real' rape. In one case where the victim had extensive bruising all over her body after being beaten and raped by two men, defence counsel's closing speech went as follows:

'There are not as many or as serious injuries as might be expected from her account. What she does have is consistent with vigorous sexual intercourse with consent, but in rather cramped conditions. ... If she had been fighting for her honour as she says she was, there would be some injury to the defendants too. The examination shows that there wasn't – no sign of injury anywhere on them.'

There are cases where the victim's injuries are so severe that it is impossible to minimise or understate them with any credibility. It may then be conceded by the defence that she had been 'unfortunate' but nevertheless argued that her physical condition after the assault was not inconsistent with consent: 'Some people prefer sex in a violent way – it was not necessarily without her consent.'

On occasions the defence goes to considerable lengths to sustain this position. In one case, for example, the victim had a vaginal tear requiring several stitches as a result of the rape and the police surgeon who examined her gave evidence that such a tearing of the tissues was extremely unlikely to occur unless considerable force was used. The defence was to dispute this view and called another doctor as an expert witness. The following is an extract from his evidence:

Medical witness: There is not a single obstetrician who has practised over five years [sic] who hasn't seen such tears as a result of consensual sexual intercourse in non-virgins. The dangers of inferring lack of consent from genital injuries are commonly taught in forensic medicine textbooks. These tears simply occur through penetration, where there is a disproportion in the size of those involved.

115

Clearly then, much effort is invested in rape trials in establishing that a victim without physical injuries is not to be believed and that even severe injuries should be interpreted with caution as they do not necessarily equate with lack of consent.

The conviction rate among men who inflicted moderate or severe physical injuries on their victims, such as extensive bruising, lacerations, tearing of tissues or fractures is 69 per cent as compared to 51 per cent among those who behaved less violently. These data clearly suggest that evidence of violence additional to the sexual assault is helpful in securing a conviction. The bruised and battered woman approximates to the stereotype of the 'ideal' rape victim more closely than the one whose sexual violation results in less marked physical injuries.

... and after

Although it is common knowledge that the vast majority of rapes go unreported because the victim is too embarrassed and ashamed to go to the police, there is also an expectation that the 'genuine' victim will be so distressed by the assault that she will report it immediately. These conflicting assumptions exist side by side, but when it comes to the law, the latter takes precedence. It has been noted earlier that one of the unique features of the law relating to rape is that evidence of an 'early complaint' is admissible at the trial. This indicates the law's assumption that if an immediate report is not essential to prove that the offence occurred, it is at least helpful in showing that the woman's behaviour was consistent with lack of consent:

The evidence [of fresh complaint] is not to be taken as proof of the facts complained of, but only as a matter to be borne in mind by the jury in considering the consistency, and therefore, the credibility, of the victim's story.[5]

Studies conducted in the USA on the social and psychological determinants of reporting behaviour in victims of rape have found that there are many reasons why women choose not to report, including embarrassment, fear of retaliation and of further ordeals, shame and a desire to avoid the stigma of being known as a rape victim. Dukes[6] studied a group of women who had been victims of rape and looked for differences between the reporters and non-reporters. He found that four main variables distinguished the two groups. One was the strength of fear experienced by the victim immediately after the rapist left: the stronger the fear, the more likely the victim was to report. The other three variables concerned the victim's impressions of police concern, efficiency and consideration in the handling of rape cases.

If similar factors apply in this country, adverse publicity over the last few years about the victim's treatment at the police station will have done little to improve women's perceptions of police consideration and is unlikely to have encouraged them to report rapes. A study by the Scottish Home and Health Department[7] indicates that a substantial majority of victims in rape cases found various aspects of the police investigation stressful. In particular, there were strong criticisms of the lack of consideration and disbelief with which the victims felt they were being treated. The same study reports that 45 per cent of the cases in their sample proceeded no further than the police stage. The Advisory Group on the Law of Rape did not consider fully the police treatment of rape victims, but urged that their questioning should be conducted in a 'tactful and sympathetic' manner and, more recently, new guidelines issued by the Home Office[8] on this subject also indicate an official acknowledgment that all is not well with the treatment victims receive at the police station. In addition, some police forces have adopted new measures aimed at improving their investigative techniques in sexual assault cases. The Metropolitan Police, for example, have recently set up systematic training programmes for officers dealing with such investigations and are currently establishing victim examination suites with special facilities for rape victims. However, the impact of these reforms on the level of reporting will probably take some time to filter through.

Whatever the reasons for it, any delay in reporting will be held against the woman at the trial. As one defence counsel put it,

'Afterwards, she doesn't go to the police or anyone in the street to complain. She doesn't complain to her mother, which would have been normal. Instead, she lies to her. Is her conduct afterwards consistent with that of a person who was raped, or who consented?

If the victim fails to report the offence for days or weeks, she is most unlikely to be believed. In cross-examination she will be asked to justify the delay and this may give the defence an opportunity to suggest the 'real' reason for what is presented as an unquestionably false complaint:

Defence counsel: Why didn't you go to the police [after the rape]?
Victim: I was too terrified ... I thought they'd be harsh ... I thought they would be very unsympathetic.
Judge: Why did you go eventually?
Victim: I felt ashamed of what had happened to me. I also thought that he might rape somebody else, or come back and rape me again.
Defence counsel: At what stage did you go to the police?
Victim: I went the day I found out about the pregnancy.
Defence counsel: I suggest you went because you wanted to blame somebody for getting you pregnant. So that you could justify your pregnancy to your relatives.

Another strategy is for the defence to set up expectations in the jury as to what happens in a 'real' rape and then to ask them to judge their case with reference to that, and to draw what is presented as the inevitable conclusion about the defendant's guilt:

Defence counsel: Consider the circumstances in which the allegation was made. Rape and indecent assault are extremely serious charges. You'd expect that an allegation of rape would be made at the earliest opportunity – because it is such outrageous conduct, in this case, by someone the victim knew. If there is any truth in it, why didn't she make a complaint the following morning? She could have gone out and complained straight after the incident. She could have complained to her neighbours. She could have told someone at work, on Friday, Saturday or Sunday. But it wasn't until Monday that she went to the Magistrates' Court [and afterwards, to the police].

When a complaint is made an hour or two after the incident, the victim may still be asked to justify this delay. In the following extract, the woman told the court that she went to the police station immediately after the rape, but there was some discrepancy between her timing and that of the police officer who first saw her. Defence counsel commented on this as follows:

'It is more than significant evidence if the complainant makes her complaint as soon as possible. There is something wrong about that in this case: it is not disputed that she arrived at the police station after 5.20pm, but she got out of the [defendant's] car at 3.50pm. We have no evidence of what happened in between.'

The jury in this case were unable to reach a verdict and a retrial was ordered. In the second trial the police produced further evidence which confirmed that the complaint was in fact made at the earlier time of 4pm and the defendant was convicted.

Defence counsel invariably refers to any delay in reporting in cross-examination and comments on it in the closing speech: not making an immediate formal complaint is sometimes referred to as 'an extraordinary thing to do', going against 'what you'd expect a girl who has been raped to do'.

Is there any systematic link between the time of reporting a rape and the verdict? The findings of this study suggest that there is. About 40 per cent of the victims reported the offence following some delay after the departure of their assailant, ranging from one day to around three months. The conviction rate for those accused of the rape of late reporters was 38 per cent, as compared to 73 per cent for those whose victims made an immediate complaint. The difference, again, is statistically significant.

So far, the various victim characteristics which appear to be associated with the defendant's conviction have been considered in isolation from each other. However, while the effect of some variables alone (e.g. consent to being in the situation) is not strong enough to have a statistically significant impact on the outcome of the trial, it may be that, coupled with one or more factors (e.g. evidence of promiscuity and no injuries) it will work against a conviction.

In order to examine the combined effect of various victim characteristics on the outcome of the trial, the clustering of these factors has been examined. The 'ideal' rape, most closely approximating to the stereotype, is one where the victim is sexually inexperienced and has a 'respectable' lifestyle, whose assailant was a stranger and whose company she had not willingly found herself in. She will have fought back, been physically hurt and, afterwards, promptly reported the offence. A further factor which seemed to favour conviction is the presence of more than one defendant. An index of factors constructed on these assumptions strongly relates to the outcome of the trial. Cases with less than two such factors present were significantly less likely to end in a conviction than those with three or more such factors – the conviction rates being 33 per cent and 72 per cent respectively.

It is also noteworthy that there were no convictions at all in the cases with no favourable factors present and no acquittals in the group which had six favourable factors present. The latter group not only seems to be invariably convicted, but usually heavier than average sentences are also imposed.

It is clear that to understand fully the different outcomes of criminal trials, one must look at a whole range of factors and not only those relating to the victim. Nevertheless, these findings clearly indicate that the characteristics of the victim have a considerable impact on whether or not the defendant in a rape trial is convicted, and that the offence of rape continues to be defined largely with reference to the deserving character of the victim, as well as to commonly held stereotypical views of the offence itself which bear little resemblance to the reality of rape for many women. The sentencing process parallels the trial and verdict in this respect and will be discussed in the following chapter.

Chapter 8

Verdict, mitigation and sentence

In view of the predominant focus on the victim in rape trials, it is hardly surprising that the conviction rate following a contested trial is abysmally low. Only 44 per cent of the eighty defendants pleading 'not guilty' in this study were convicted of rape, attempted rape or aiding and abetting rape. The Court of Appeal, for various reasons, subsequently quashed three of these convictions. A further 8 per cent were found guilty of indecent assault, but not guilty of rape. Retrials were ordered for 2 per cent of the accused, as the jury were unable to reach a verdict the first time round. The remaining 46 per cent were cleared of all charges.

As for the offenders who pleaded guilty, almost a third denied the main rape charge but admitted to another sexual offence – usually indecent assault or unlawful sexual intercourse and, very occasionally, incest – and were sentenced on that basis.[1] Although the remainder of this chapter is only concerned with sentencing for rape offences, two points must be made here.

First, the 'lesser' sexual offence that men accused of rape are most often convicted of is indecent assault, for which the maximum penalty at the time of this study was two years' imprisonment.[2] Very few of the offenders received this maximum sentence. Second, a high proportion of those charged with rape whose guilty plea is accepted actually plead to alternative counts of less serious offences. This finding constitutes a serious challenge to the commonly asserted claim that plea bargaining has no place in English justice.

What were the penalties meted out to men convicted of rape offences in this study? With the exception of a single offender, they were all sentenced to borstal or immediate imprisonment. The exception was a suspended sentence passed on a man who admitted raping a woman and fleeing the country immediately afterwards.

He was captured on his return here some two or three years later. Why the delay in bringing him to justice should justify a suspended sentence was not altogether clear and had there happened to be a reporter in court at the time, the case may well have precipitated another of the public outcries that, understandably, plague this area of the criminal justice system.

In 1982, as a direct result of a case where a judge imposed a £2,000 fine on a man convicted of rape, the Lord Chief Justice issued new, if somewhat limited, guidelines on sentencing in rape cases. The gist of these was that unless 'wholly exceptional' circumstances were present, rape should always be punished by immediate imprisonment, for the following reasons:

First of all, to mark the gravity of the offence. Secondly, to emphasise public disapproval. Thirdly, to serve as a warning to others. Fourthly to punish the offender, and last, but by no means least, to protect women.[3]

There has only been one case reported to date where 'wholly exceptional' circumstances were found to be present and where the Court of Appeal substituted a probation order for the term of imprisonment originally imposed by the trial judge.[4] That case involved an offender described as mentally retarded and a victim suffering from Down's Syndrome. The Court of Appeal decided that the incident was more akin to indecent assault than rape and that the man had only a child-like understanding of the gravity of his actions. The last factor taken into account is a great deal more questionable: the Court commented that although the victim was clearly not consenting, the low level of protest she made 'because of her physical defects' also contributed to making the circumstances 'wholly exceptional' in this case.

The 1982 guidelines did not go so far as to suggest how long a period of imprisonment might reasonably achieve the four-fold aim stated above; however, they did specify a number of features which may aggravate the crime. These include the use of a weapon, of brutal threats and excessive violence; serious mental or physical injury to the victim; a very young or elderly victim; additional sexual indignities; an offender in a position of trust vis-à-vis his victim; intrusion into the victim's home; holding the victim captive for a period of time; a series of rapes, or a gang rape.

As mentioned above, the vast majority of convicted rapists in this study did go to prison. But what of the level of sentencing? Omitting five youngsters who were sent to borstal, nearly 60 per cent of those imprisoned got less than four years, with over 40 per cent receiving a sentence in the most common range which is somewhere between two and four years. The maximum penalty of life imprisonment, often quoted to juries as a measure of the seriousness of the offence, was given to four offenders, representing 8 per cent of those imprisoned for rape. The overall distribution

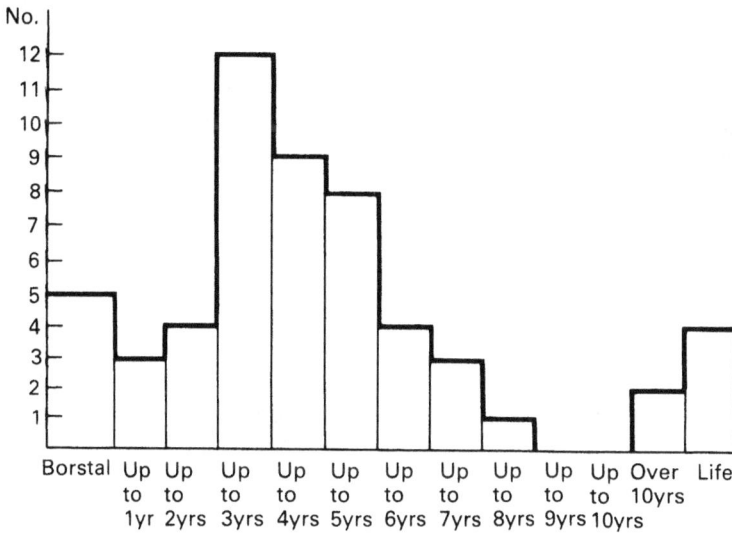

N=55, excluding one person convicted of rape in the sample who received a suspended sentence

Figure 8.1: *Length of imprisonment for rape offences*

of sentences is shown in Figure 8.1. A comparison with *Criminal Statistics* shows that these sentences are broadly in line with the general level of sentencing for rape offences in England and Wales for the year of study.

The level of sentencing is one of the most fiercely criticised aspects of the courts' dealings with rape. This is of course particularly true when a non-custodial sentence is given, but the length of sentence is also criticised as being totally inadequate for an offence of this gravity. In November 1985, six teenage members of a South London gang were sentenced to youth custody ranging from three to seven years for the rape of two young girls. The girls had been chased, caught and robbed, frogmarched to some garages under a block of flats and raped many times over by the whole gang. To add insult to injury, the boys laughed and joked while they were waiting for their turn and gave running commentaries to one another. The judge's comments in the case conveyed that he at least regarded these sentences as exemplary, 'to express society's horror of the mounting volume of man's inhumanity to women'.[5] He was strongly criticised by the popular press for passing sentences considered derisory in view of the particularly vicious nature of the attacks. Feelings about this case ran sufficiently high for a Member of Parliament to call for the judge's resignation, a proposition for which he was thoroughly rebuked by the Lord Chancellor.

In fact, sentences of seven years on teenagers with no previous convictions for similar offences are quite standard within the range of sentences for rape. Had the judge passed a harsher sentence, this would almost certainly have been reduced by the Court of Appeal.

The tariff for rape

It has been argued that the process of working out an appropriate sentence for any criminal offence involves three stages. The process begins with the definition of a scale of sentences in relation to typical instances within the offence category. Second, the appropriate level of sentence for the facts of the particular offence is identified somewhere along that general scale. Finally, allowance is made for various characteristics of the offender which may reduce the sentence below that level. Taking the offender as well as the offence into account is a relatively new development which emerged only during the course of this century.

The first stage of the sentencing process is 'fixed' in the sense that it is determined with reference to previous decisions: the Court of Appeal has become a major decision-making body on the principles and practice of sentencing, despite the fact that it deals only with a selection of cases, namely those where the sentence of the lower court is considered too severe. These decisions and the principles underlying them for different categories of offence have been analysed by Thomas, in a book published some years ago which has become the lawyer's sentencing bible.[6]

According to this, the range of sentences for rape goes from a usual minimum of two years to a usual maximum of twelve, with life imprisonment being reserved for a special category of offenders. In general, the maximum penalty is used only for men who have committed a very serious rape (not infrequently, a series of rapes) and who suffer from some personality disorder or instability which, in the opinion of the experts, makes them likely to do it again. Thomas makes the point that it is not normally seen as a deterrent sentence – rather, it is frequently described as a 'more merciful alternative than a long fixed term'.

For the rest, sentences of two to three years (or borstal for under 21s) are usually given where a relatively young man has raped one of his contemporaries, with minimal force and 'the victim's consent to some degree of familiarity'. The Court of Appeal normally upholds sentences of between three and five years in cases not distinguished either by the above characteristics or by aggravating factors. A sentence in excess of five years is unlikely to be upheld unless there are aggravating factors, such as rape by a group, abduction or imprisonment of the victim, other sexual abuse, etc. The scale then goes up with increasing numbers of aggravating factors, with sentences above eight years reserved for cases involving a combination of such factors 'in their strongest forms'. Twelve years seems to be the upper limit of the scale.

It is broadly within these limits that judges operate when they come to a decision as to the seriousness and the right penalty for any particular offence. Defence counsel's speech in mitigation bears on this, as it does on the third stage, which concerns the offender's circumstances. Although at this point, the defendant's guilt in the legal sense is no longer in dispute, his counsel puts forward arguments on his behalf which would tend to minimise the seriousness of the offence, the level of the defendant's responsibility for it or both. Barristers see their role in mitigation as getting the most lenient sentence possible for their clients. They are free to bring up anything at all, subject to the judge's discretion, and anything considered relevant by the judge may influence the sentence. The procedure is effectively weighted in favour of the defence. The following section discusses some of the main arguments put forward in this context, beginning with factors pertaining to the accused and going on to the definition of aggravating and mitigating factors in determining the seriousness of any particular offence.

The denial of responsibility

Mitigation bearing on the absolute responsibility of the accused for any particular offence falls into a number of categories. The main points that may be brought up in his favour are his age and history, both in terms of previous convictions and psychiatric condition; his emotional state at the time of the offence; the indirect effect of his conviction on his family or job prospects, for example; and evidence of remorse. All these may be brought up in the context of any other offence too, but there is one additional category much used in rape cases and that is the offender's sexual drive. These factors will now be explored in turn.

There is an assumption that age is a major mitigating factor: boys in their early teens are not seen as having the same responsibility for their actions as their older counterparts. Lack of maturity is used to explain both the offender's motivation ('his exceptional immaturity is the root cause of what makes him commit these offences') and his lack of understanding of the seriousness of his misbehaviour ('he was very young – he did not realise the full wickedness of his conduct at the time'). Of course, the greater protection of young offenders is a general principle of law and applies whatever crime they are convicted of.

As far as the offender's history is concerned, a variety of (apparently contradictory) factors may be drawn upon in mitigation. Good and bad records seem equally useful in this context. If he has no previous convictions, it may be argued on his behalf that this is a good sign for the future. Other indicators of decency, reliability and stability may also be introduced. Offenders are referred to as 'hard working family men' and as usually 'very kind and gentle with women'. A lay preacher, convicted of raping one of his flock, had his previous good works extensively praised in mitigation. It is sometimes difficult to escape the conclusion that defence counsel are grasping at straws at this stage: for example, one man convicted of indecently assaulting his daughter was described as an 'otherwise very good father'.

If the offender has previous convictions for other crimes, it may be argued that rape is totally out of character – this was even put forward in a case where the man had previously spent time in prison for grievous bodily harm. Amazingly, the argument that the offender is basically a good man is even put forward in cases where he has a string of convictions for sexual offences. One man who had a dreadful record for serious sexual offences against children had this said in his favour: 'Apart from a weakness with children, he is a hard working man, who has built up his own firm. He even gained a degree in classics during his last spell in prison.'

For other offenders, it is a deprived and unhappy background that is used to mitigate the offence. Emotional insecurity, social isolation, material deprivation and parental neglect in childhood may be mentioned as factors to be taken into account. While a discussion of psychiatric problems is, as expected, usually reserved for those men who are heading for a life sentence, it may also occur in cases where a short fixed sentence is being argued for. Offenders in this category were variously described as having a 'personality disorder', a 'history of psychiatric treatment' or as being on the way to 'becoming a psychopathic personality'.

Another mitigating factor that crops up with great regularity is that the man involved would never have committed such an offence had he not been under great emotional stress at the time. The implication is that he snapped under intense domestic or work pressures, but that he would not normally behave in this way. One defendant's father, for example, was called to give evidence that his son had only been in trouble since he, the father, left his wife. Another man, according to his counsel, 'would never have acted like this if business pressures had not been so intense, and if, as a result, his relationship with his wife had been less strained'. Increased alcohol consumption is often thought to be an extra factor along this dimension.

The offender's sexual drive is very often presented as the main motivating factor. It is not surprising that this is brought up so regularly, given that the mythology of rape places uncontrollable sexual urges in a prominent position as far as motivations for the offence are concerned.

There are at least two strands to this particular explanation for the crime. First, there is an appeal to sympathy for young, inexperienced boys who were simply motivated by sexual curiosity – they did not plan to commit rape, it was simply that they got carried away, the situation 'got out of hand' and the offences were committed on the spur of the moment. The message is that boys will be boys and should not be punished too severely for such misconduct.

The second approach is more directly based on the idea that men are actually controlled by their sexual drive and can only be blamed to a very limited extent for failing to subdue this strong physiological urge. Offenders may be described as showing sexual development 'well above average for their age', as victims 'of carnal desire', as 'unable to control' themselves, as 'succumbing to the temptation' and as irrevocably affected by pornographic films. Even worse, one man was said to have been 'sexually attracted' to his daughters because of his love and attraction for his wife. One barrister confidently assured the court that his client, just convicted of an attempted rape on a child, was most unlikely to do this again because of his declining sexual potency. He was in fact over 60 when he committed the offence and not much older at the time of the trial.

What is more surprising is the extent to which such arguments appear to find credence with both trial judges and judges of the Court of Appeal. Despite extensive research evidence indicating the relatively minor role of sexual motivation in rape,[7] judges often endorse the assumption that men who rape are driven by a physiological urge which they cannot control. As one Court of Appeal judgment put it, 'the facts of the offence indicated, as indeed the vast majority of offences of rape indicate, that he was a man of considerable sexual drive'.[8] The case which led to this pronouncement involved a victim who was two-and-a-half years old.

The offender's attitude to the offence and the effects of the conviction and sentence on his immediate circumstances are also used in mitigation. Any expression of remorse is extremely favourable to the offender. A guilty plea is always taken into account and some reduction in sentence allowed. This, of course, saves the victim being dragged through the courts which, as this book has shown, is a considerable bonus. Other indicators of remorse and regret include the offender's acknowledgment that only he, and not his victim, is to blame, his offer to pay compensation and, most important of all, his cooperation with the police and admissions made soon after his arrest.

A final set of mitigating factors concerns the penalty already paid by the offender in various ways. He has suffered enough already, the argument goes, and this justifies some reduction in the sentence. The career prospects of some offenders are seriously threatened by their offence: 'he has been expelled from college', said one barrister; 'he has been dismissed from his employment because of this', said another. A man who indecently assaulted a disabled girl in his professional care was said to have had his career ruined by the whole affair. As his counsel said, and one can only hope that he was right, 'he'll never get another job like this again'.

Other men are said to have been punished by the effect the crime has had on their family life. It is not uncommon for a woman to leave her husband when he has committed rape; and neither is it uncommon for families to break up when the man is convicted of sexual offences against his young daughters. Although these developments, as the job losses referred to above, come about as a direct result of the offence, it is often argued that they too justify some reduction in the sentence.

All the above factors are used to convey the notion that although the man in the dock did commit rape offences, he was not altogether blameworthy for various reasons. The plea is that there were acceptable reasons for it, which minimise his responsibility, and justify a lenient sentence. Next, we shall consider how the seriousness of the offence itself is mitigated.

The denial of harm

Defence counsel's efforts to mitigate the seriousness of the offence are strongly reminiscent of the general flavour of the cross-examination of victims in rape cases. Subtle and not so subtle criticisms of the victim abound and factors such as her sexual experience, her previous relationship with the accused, her perceived provocation of the offence and her lack of injuries may all be argued to mitigate the gravity of the offence.

It is crystal clear that the rape of women or girls with previous sexual experience is, by definition, thought to be less serious than the rape of virgins. But the assumption goes even beyond this fairly objective criterion and, on occasions, child victims are described as 'very mature for their age' or as 'sexually precocious'. The fact that such matters are raised in mitigation may be interpreted in a number of ways: it may be that relative sexual maturity in a child is believed to excuse the offender's aproach to her; or, and this seemed to be the most favoured interpretation, it may be that when a child is not totally innocent before the offence, the seriousness of the rape diminishes somewhat. As one counsel said, in commenting on two victims aged 10 and 12 respectively at the time of the offence, 'The girls were experienced when he came to them – he didn't actually corrupt them.'

The assumption that there is only so much damage you can do to already damaged goods is much stronger when it comes to women with a more readily identifiable and greater degree of sexual experience. The morality of the victim is always commented on, at least in passing: she may be described as having 'considerable sexual experience', on the assumption that one more partner, even if she did not consent, really cannot have done her great harm. One barrister commented that the rape in question was 'not the gravest of acts, when one comes to consider the parties involved' – the victims were two prostitutes. For other lawyers, the identity of the victim seems to define the existence of the crime itself: a barrister whose client had been convicted of attempted rape had this to say: 'This is not really a rape – things went wrong with a prostitute.'

The victim's previous relationship with the defendant is also a major factor and not only when the previous relationship had at one point been a sexual one. In a gang rape involving six men, one of the offenders had a prior passing acquaintance with the victim. His counsel argued that 'he was in a situation slightly different from the others, in that he was slightly known to the complainant'. In another case, the defendant was described as having had 'a former relationship of sorts with the girl'. In both instances, the existence of such a relationship, however remote, was argued to mitigate the rape.

And now for provocation. Judge Richards is not the only member of the legal profession to refer to the contributory negligence of a victim of rape – the very same phrase, long before it became publicized, was extensively used in mitigation in the Old Bailey cases. This is raised in the belief that provocation or consent to some familiarity by the victim contribute to making the offence less serious than it would otherwise have been. If the victim went willingly to the place where the rape occurred, she was said to have given 'partial consent'. If she went for a drink with the man and kissed him, she was said to have given him 'an open invitation' and to have 'egged him on'. If she flirted with him, but refused intercourse and he ended up raping her at knifepoint, her behaviour was described as one 'of clear provocation'.

The presence of injuries is a major determinant of the perceived gravity of any rape offence. In mitigation, there are three principal ways of minimising such injuries. The first is to stress the absence of physical injury or to underplay its seriousness. It is often said that no 'force or violence' was used, or that the 'rape was not as brutal as it might have been'. The term 'no serious violence' is sometimes applied in cases where, according to defence counsel himself, there were 'slapping and blows rather than battering'.

Arguments of this nature may also be put forward on behalf of defendants whose self-confessed verbal threats would have terrified most women: one offender, for example, threatened to put a lit candle inside his victim if she struggled; the fact that he did not actually beat her as well was argued to go to his credit when it came to mitigation.

The second strategy is to argue that the psychological damage suffered by the victim was not long lasting and that she had fully recovered by the time of the trial. Any assessment of such recovery is entirely based on the observed behaviour of the victim in the witness box, rather than any medical or expert evidence. When a victim is not obviously hysterical while she is giving evidence, barristers are rather hasty to conclude that she has 'recovered from the psychological point of view', that 'she does not appear to have been disturbed by it', that 'she has recovered a certain poise', or that 'she hasn't been badly affected'.

The third strategy consists in showing that the rape was not as bad as it might have been because the defendant was not entirely devoid of humanity in his treatment of the victim. In this context, it may be argued that a man stopped having regular intercourse with his daughters when they turned 14; that the offender tried to stop the victim from jumping out of the window as she was trying to escape him; and that after raping and robbing the victim, he left her enough money for her fare home.

It is not easy to ascertain how persuasive these various arguments are and what impact they have on the sentencing process. While judges frequently give an indication of what mitigating factors they find acceptable, it is impossible to ascertain systematically how many months are taken off for a guilty plea and how many for a provocative victim. This is partly due to the nature of the data here and partly to the fact that judges consider a combination of all the factors present in any case – the impact of any individual item cannot be determined in isolation. In addition, decisions will vary from one judge to another. Nevertheless, a consideration of these factors and the weight they are accorded in Court of Appeal decisions is revealing and appears to show that the criteria used to determine the gravity of any particular offence are based on highly questionable assumptions.

The determinants of gravity

According to Thomas, the victim's previous sexual experience is not a major factor in sentencing. In support of this contention, he cites a Court of Appeal judgment which goes as follows: 'it is not to be thought that whenever the victim of rape is a woman of experience or of dubious moral standards it is any less an outrage to take that which the woman is not willing to give'.[9]

However, a reading of reported Court of Appeal cases shows that, at least as a background factor, some comment about the victim's sexual history almost invariably appears in the text. This is true whether it is the presence or absence of sexual experience which is being emphasised. The sexual innocence of victims is pointed out in ways which make it quite clear that they are not blamed for any part of the offence. They may be described as 'single and without sexual experience',[10] as 'a girl of only 13 who was a virgin'[11] or as 'a girl of irreproachable character'.[12] This may be contrasted with descriptions of victims whose past behaviour was less exemplary, where the text of the judgment contains references to victims as 'age 31, sexually experienced, living there with her boyfriend',[13] and as a married woman who had a boyfriend.[14] In one case, the victim of a gang rape was even more elaborately portrayed as follows:

The victim was a girl of 15, who, let it be said, was a very experienced young woman for her age. She was on the pill and admitted that she had had sexual intercourse many times with different people, at least from the age of 14.[15]

There are no reported cases which explicitly state that the victim's prior sexual experience was taken into account by the Court of Appeal in reducing or upholding a sentence. There can be little doubt, however, that descriptions of victims in the above terms reflect some notion that prior virginity or promiscuity are of some relevance at least in determining the seriousness of the offence.

The existence of a prior non-sexual relationship between the offender and the victim does not appear to affect Court of Appeal sentencing decisions. The position regarding a previous sexual relationship is unclear and reveals some inconsistencies. One decision takes the view that the existence of a previous sexual relationship between the offender and the victim is not a reason for reducing a sentence of three years.[16] Yet when it comes to the rape of ex-wives, sentences have been reduced on the grounds that

this was not the rape of a stranger but of a woman with whom the appellant had lived for ten years, for this reason, and because he had pleaded guilty, although a sentence of imprisonment must follow a conviction for rape in all but exceptional circumstances, the sentence could be put at the lowest end of the bracket.... This [previous marriage] does add a different dimension to the case.[17]

The sentence was reduced from three to two years. In another case, the submission that the existence in the past of a marriage 'during which sexual intercourse would have taken place regularly and normally' should be grounds to reduce a sentence of four years were rejected and the sentence upheld.[18]

Thomas's analysis reveals that the behaviour on the

part of the victim which increases the risk of rape, such as willing participation in minor sexual activity or (to a lesser extent) imprudent behaviour such as accepting a lift in a car from strangers, is usually treated as a reason for some reduction in sentence.[19]

This is another area where the Court of Appeal has been somewhat inconsistent. In 1979, it upheld a term of five years' imprisonment for a rape accompanied by considerable violence, although counsel for the appellant had suggested that something should be taken off for the fact that she allowed some familiarity before refusing consent to intercourse. The Court felt that prior familiarity did not mitigate.[20] Two years later, a man was also sentenced to five years at the Crown Court after raping at knifepoint a woman who invited him to spend an evening in her flat. On that occasion, the Court was persuaded to reduce the sentence substantially on the following grounds:

We acknowledge the seriousness of what the appellant did ... But it does not come within the class of rape in which a woman has been put into the position of succumbing to rape by the use of force of one kind or another by a man who has suddenly come upon her and who has injured her physically as well as mentally and who has shown no contrition whatever, and who is a man of ill character. There is much to be said for the view that the appellant thought that by being invited into the lady's home that evening, they being separated from their respective spouses would go rather further in their relationship than spending a quiet evening together watching television. For some reason best known to himself, he did something which was foreign to his nature; he picked up a knife and used it to her with the effect which has been described. Having regard to all those matters, we think that there is sufficient mitigation here to enable us to reduce quite markedly the sentence that was imposed. Our decision is that we can do justice by quashing the sentence of five years' imprisonment and replacing it by one of three years' imprisonment.[21]

How far is physical violence taken into account? It is clearly assumed, and this is one point on which the Court of Appeal is fairly consistent, that rape by violence is worse than rape by threats:

the rape was not the most serious of its kind, being a rape by threat rather than by actual physical beating; there was no other violence than was necessary to complete the rape.[22]

While in general, the length of sentence goes up with the degree of violence used, it is also true to say that physical violence is sometimes underplayed, particularly when it leaves no lasting physical marks − a questionable practice. There might well be criticism of the Court of Appeal's view that 'no grave violence' was used in a case where the man tore some strips from a sheet, tied his victim's hands and feet and gagged her. The lack of 'grave violence' was used as the main justification for reducing the five-year sentence to three years.[23]

Conclusion

In arriving at an appropriate sentence for any particular offence, judges aim to meet several objectives, including the punishment of the offender, the protection of the public and the expression of society's disapproval of the crime. Current sentencing practice for rape may be criticised on two main grounds. First, the level of punishment often dispensed is inadequate to meet the above objectives, or to persuade victims that it is worthwhile for them to seek justice through the courts. Second, sentencing practice is inconsistent and based at least partly on unacceptable criteria for determining the seriousness of the offence.

Some have argued that a mandatory prison sentence for rape is a possible way of increasing the protection afforded by the criminal justice system to women with respect to rape. However, it has also been observed that a mandatory sentence might encourage plea bargains where defendants plead guilty to a lesser charge for which they might escape imprisonment. In any event, the Court of Appeal's 1982 sentencing guidelines reflect a commitment to the principle that rape should normally be punished by immediate imprisonment.

There are, under the current law, very real difficulties involved in ensuring that within the context of this general principle terms of imprisonment are adequate to deal with the gravity of the offence in each case. Judges who pass draconian sentences are very likely to have them slashed by the Court of Appeal. To give just one example: in 1981, a fifteen-year sentence on a man, acting in concert with another, for the rape and buggery of a woman who had been forcibly taken to the place where the offences were committed was considered 'far too high and wrong in principle'[24] and reduced to eight years.

On the other hand, nothing much can be done about judges who err on the side of leniency. They may make the headlines for a couple of days or, if the circumstances are really bizarre, the Lord Chancellor or the Lord Chief Justice may have a private word with them. But the prosecution has no right of appeal against an over-lenient sentence, and this is an area where reform has been advocated in previous years, against fierce opposition from the judiciary.

The second important issue concerns criteria currently used to determine the seriousness of particular rape offences. The range of penalties, as we have seen, is extremely wide; yet there are no degrees of rape in law. The essential ingredient of the offence, sexual intercourse without consent, is present in all instances. Thus, it is the circumstances surrounding the individual crime that determine its seriousness for sentencing purposes.

Those circumstances must be very carefully considered to ensure that factors eventually taken into account are relevant in a true and acceptable sense. The 1982 sentencing guidelines are of considerable help, establishing as they do a number of well thought out aggravating factors. Some of these are subject to interpretation, which may cause problems in certain cases: for example, it will be remembered that one aggravating factor is the abuse of a relationship of trust between the offender and the victim. In at least one case to date, the Court of Appeal found no such factor was present in a case where a man invited an acquaintance to a party to celebrate the birth of his daughter – there was no party, as he well knew, and he raped her.[25] It would seem highly reasonable to interpret this as breach of trust.

But the most important point to be made here is that while there are circumstances which add to the horror of non-consensual sex, as the use of the term 'aggravating factor' conveys, nothing can take away from its seriousness. Rape is a particularly vile form of assault, which often inflicts long-term emotional harm. The anxiety, confusion and loss of confidence that arise in its aftermath may take months or years to abate. The fact that the victim was sexually experienced beforehand does not detract from its gravity. The fact that she and the offender knew one another, or even had had consensual intercourse in the past, does not make it less serious. As for contributory negligence, it is invidious to suggest that if the victim is a woman travelling alone late at night or hitchhiking, her victimisation becomes trivial. Great harm can and has been done by the suggestion that there are circumstances which make rape a petty offence.

It is essential that a more rational sentencing policy in rape be encouraged, both in terms of the penalties inflicted and in terms of the factors used to determine the gravity of the offence. Discrepancies between sentences given to convicted rapists should reflect the presence or absence of aggravating factors and not judgments about the victim's perceived responsibility for the offence or that she got no more than she deserved.

Chapter 9

The lesson from abroad

Over the last ten years or so, legal and academic commentators in the USA, Canada, Australia and elsewhere have also drawn attention to the inadequacies of their own legal systems in their dealings with rape. Most of the criticism, as in this country, has been directed at the routine admission of evidence of the victim's sexual behaviour before the rape. It has invariably been argued that this is irrelevant to her credibility, rarely relevant to consent, highly prejudicial for the prosecution's case and humiliating for the woman concerned. In many cases, the concern with the legal treatment of rape victims prompted the setting up of various groups and commissions to consider the problem, and subsequently, legislative reform.

In the USA, the trend towards legal reform began in the early 1970s and almost every state has by now modified its rape laws. The new laws vary greatly from state to state, both in their substance and complexity, but a central provision everywhere is to limit the defence lawyer's ability to enquire into the victim's sexual past. The range of procedures adopted to this end ranges from virtually total prohibition to unfettered judicial discretion not dissimilar to the English model. For example, in Texas, any sexual history evidence whatsoever is admitted if, and to the extent that, the judge believes its 'probative value to exceed its prejudice'.[1] New York has another popular version of the discretionary approach, which states that, in general, evidence of this sort will be excluded, goes on to list specific exemptions and ends with a catch-all provision allowing in anything 'determined by the court ... to be relevant and admissible in the interests of justice'.[2]

Some states distinguish between sexual history evidence brought in to discredit the victim and evidence which may affect the issue in the trial. Some statutes refer to sexual conduct and specific sexual acts and others to sexual reputation – a distinction of considerable significance. Some states impose time limits, usually of one year, and bar any evidence of sexual character before that time. Not all of these reforms have been well received. As one commentator observed, some of the variations

present practical or even constitutional problems. Unhappily, many reform efforts, well-meant but ill-conceived, pose more dilemmas than they resolve.[3]

Most of the Australian states have also introduced legislative reform in this area. Evidence of sexual experience is controlled in different ways, but all the states adopt an essentially discretionary approach. Some exclude the evidence if it is only relevant to credibility, but otherwise leave the question to the judge who may decide to let it in if he finds it 'in all the circumstances of the case, justified'.[4] Elsewhere, sexual history evidence can be admitted if the court thinks it is of 'substantial relevance to the facts in issue',[5] or 'desirable in the interests of justice'.[6] The New South Wales provisions in general prohibit the admission of sexual conduct evidence except in specific instances. It allows evidence to be admitted where it relates to sexual experience (or lack of it) around the time of the alleged offence, and to events which form part of the circumstances in which it was committed; or where it is evidence of the allegation being made after the discovery of pregnancy or disease.[7]

Thus, the majority of the new US and Australian statutes adopt a formula which ensures that discretion remains firmly with the judiciary. This may partly be due to the fact that when faced with the task of forecasting every possible case where the admission of sexual history evidence might be just and appropriate, legislators have tended to take the easier option by deciding on discretion as the best course. And if the law does no more than advise the judge to balance relevance against prejudice in making these decisions, there can certainly be no suggestion that the defendant's rights are being eroded. How are these schemes working out in other contexts?

The consequence of discretion

It is somewhat surprising that the impact of the wide range of reforms introduced in the USA in the 1970s has not been more systematically monitored. Such research evidence as there is, however, strongly suggests that there is little difference between conviction rates for rape in states with traditional rape legislation and states where substantial reforms have been enacted. But perhaps the biggest empirical blow to the effectiveness of discretionary reforms comes from a study by Borgida and White. They conducted a large-scale jury simulation experiment to examine the impact of legal process on inferences made by the jury under different legislative procedures governing the admission of sexual history evidence. They distinguished three types of legislatures: first, common law; second, 'moderate reform' which refers to legislatures that had changed their law but left its interpretation in the hands of judges – what I have termed discretionary schemes; and third, 'radical reform', where the admissibility of sexual history evidence is clearly defined in legislation and where little or nothing is left to the personal judgment of the trial judge.

Not surprisingly, they found that only the 'radical reform' rule seemed to restrict juries' inference of consent and to increase the victim's credibility as well as the likelihood of conviction. However, even that applied only in cases where other features were unlikely to suggest consent or contributory behaviour. The authors also concluded, rather disturbingly, that there is nothing to distinguish 'moderate reform' from 'common law' rules:

A particularly distressing aspect of this pattern ... is that the impact of prior sexual history evidence with moderate reform and common law rules in an otherwise improbable consent case is apparently detrimental to the prosecution's case[8].

There are of course limits to how much can be inferred from simulated jury studies, but other evidence also suggests that discretionary schemes tend to run into trouble in other jurisdictions. Their shortcomings are clearly illustrated, for example, by the implementation of the Evidence Act Amendment Act of South Australia. Like our own law reform, this was passed in 1976 and was far from being a radical piece of legislation. In fact, it has been much criticised for being muddled and confusing. Be that as it may, this legislation provides that evidence of sexual morality or sexual conduct can be admitted only with the permission of the trial judge, if he is satisfied that the admission of the evidence is justified. The South Australian provision has been extensively analysed by the courts and the results of this analysis have been summarised by Aronson, Raeburn and Weinberg.[9] These commentators found that there is a great deal of judicial mistrust of the relevant section, sometimes to the point of hostility. While it represents no more than a very limited restriction on indiscriminate cross-examination, one judge commented on it as follows:

The section in its present form presents the rather disturbing prospect of an innocent man being in danger of being convicted because he is unable to practise the right given to him at common law to cross-examine the party who seeks to have him convicted of what is a very serious crime.[10]

This is rather reminiscent of the remarks some English judges have made about Section 2 here. In addition, judges in South Australia have found ways of neutralising the impact of legislative reform by ensuring that almost any sexual history evidence gets in. In one much quoted judgment, the Chief Justice spoke of the 'numerous situations in which evidence of sexual experiences or sexual morality may be relevant to one of the factual issues in the case'[11] and provided a long list of examples. These include cases where the defendant alleges that the woman is accusing him of rape because he refused to give her money: 'It is relevant to inquire whether she was in the habit of obtaining or asking for money in return for intercourse.' There is no indication that supporting evidence would be required before such questions are allowed. Another instance where sexual history may be relevant is where the complainant is 'experienced or sophisticated' and the defence is consent: questions about her sexual past may provide a test of the truth of her account of the details of the alleged crime. The reaction of such a woman in a sexual situation, it is said, may be expected to differ from that of an unsophisticated and inexperienced girl. It is not said how. But the net effect is that defence counsel is allowed to delve into the woman's sexual past to show, as Temkin has argued, that so experienced a woman is unlikely to have found herself trapped in the situation she describes. We are back to the myth that sexually experienced women do not get raped or that a woman with experience is more likely to have consented. There can be few loopholes of judicial discretion to rival this one.[12]

The Chief Justice also stated that it would not always be possible to restrict cross-examination to specific aspects of the victim's sexual past and envisaged that in general 'once the gate is opened the whole field [would be] liable to survey'.[13]

Both informal and formal sources attest to the disappointing effect of restricting legislation. South Australian women, initially enthusiastic about the reforms, monitored the outcome of particular cases and feel that the legislation has had no practical effect at all. They suggest that the only change since law reform is that cases take longer because the defence lawyer must formally ask for permission to do what he previously did automatically.[14] The Director of the New South Wales Criminal Law Review Division agrees that the provision of a discretionary rule in South Australian legislation 'has not satisfactorily changed the pre-existing law and practice in relation to prior sexual behaviour'.[15]

And although the impact of other discretionary schemes has not been studied in quite so much detail, there are strong indications that they have also failed to bring about any change in other Australian states. Raw data about the frequency and success of formal applications under the Victorian legislation indicates that approximately 70 per cent of these were successful.[16]

In Western Australia, assertions that law reform has done nothing to improve the victim's negative experiences in pursuing a rape complaint through the legal system are supported by the findings of an empirical study which examined rape trials before and after reform. Newby[17] studied transcripts from all rape trials heard in the Supreme Court of Western Australia from 1974 to 1979 in order to determine what sexual history evidence was admitted before law reform and whether evidence was held inadmissible after reform. A preliminary report based on part of these data reveals that the operation of the Western Australian reforms is not dissimilar to that of the Sexual Offences (Amendment) Act 1976 here. In each of the cases after reform where the defence considered it necessary to produce such evidence, permission was granted – in some cases, without any requirement on defence counsel to show 'substantial relevance'. Newby gives the example of a case where defence counsel got permission to introduce evidence that the 16-year-old complainant was not a virgin, apparently to 'counteract the effect of her youthful and innocent appearance'. Elsewhere, evidence was introduced through the 'back door', in terms of conversations the victim was alleged to have had with the defendant about her sexual experiences.

Thus, evidence from a variety of disparate sources unequivocally indicates that discretionary schemes aiming to restrict the admission of the victim's past in a rape trial do not work. Problems of subjective interpretation override any concern with the victim's treatment and legislation passed with the sole aim of improving her experience in court is effectively disregarded and re-interpreted by the judiciary. There is now increasing agreement that discretionary legislation has not had the hoped-for effect in bringing about major changes in the criminal justice system's dealing with rape. Even the supporters of discretionary provisions concede that courts may be far too ready to assume that any past sexual activity by a woman makes her more likely to consent to any sexual activity.

There is clearly a genuine problem in charting a course between inflexible legislative rules and totally unfettered judicial discretion. In some jurisdictions, legislators decided not to take any chances with the judges and passed laws which strictly define the scope of what is and is not acceptable when it comes to a rape victim's cross-examination. Have these schemes been any more effective in bringing about improvement in the experience of rape victims in court?

The impact of radical reform

It must be said at the outset that legislative reforms which may be called radical in this sense are in the minority, certainly in the first wave of new provisions which emerged in the 1970s. Only one such American scheme in Michigan has been extensively described and monitored, but such evidence as is available suggests that this kind of reform is considerably more likely to achieve its aims than are discretionary provisions.

Law reform introduced in Michigan was extensive and sometimes controversial.[18] Under the new provisions, sexual assault law became 'sex-neutral', in the sense that it now allows both men and women to be both offenders and victims. Degrees of sexual assault were defined and the previously confusing overlap between offences such as rape, gross indecency, etc. eliminated. Proof of physical force is not required to secure a conviction. Husbands are no longer exempt from rape prosecution provided the couple are living apart or one of them has filed for a divorce. The new law also does away with the need for corroboration which was previously required in rape cases.

Under its old law, Michigan was in the same position as most other jurisdictions at that date with regard to admitting evidence of the victim's previous sexual activities. The reform removes judicial discretion and substitutes a statutory prohibition which, according to the law's supporters, does nothing to interfere with the defendant's rights but merely ensures that highly inflammatory and irrelevant matters are not brought up in court. It does nothing more than to put defendants in rape and other criminal trials on the same footing:

The reform does take away from defendants in rape cases an opportunity not available to defendants in any other case to escape punishment by the stratagem of smearing the victim's reputation and making her previous personal life the key and deciding issue in the case. But the reform does not deny to rape defendants any opportunity now accorded persons charged with other crimes.[19]

The emphasis is then on making rape law provisions similar to those of other criminal law, rather than singling out rape for special treatment. The new statute expressly prohibits evidence of sexual past with two very specific exceptions which are subject to the judge's decision in each case. The first exception concerns her prior sexual activities with the accused; the second concerns evidence of specific instances of sexual activity showing 'the course or origin of semen, pregnancy or disease'. In both cases the judge has to consider whether any such evidence is relevant to the issue in the case and whether its prejudicial nature outweighs its probative value before coming to a decision.

The new law has not had a smooth passage: its constitutionality has been challenged in the Michigan Appeal Courts and so far most judges have upheld the constitutionality of reform. But as the law's principal drafter, Virginia Nordby, notes,

opposing considerations are still surfacing and being mulled over by appellate judges, some of whom are surely postponing final judgment until they are presented with more varied fact situations.... In sum, the law is still in flux ... But courts are clearly committed to preserving the legislative policy except in extreme circumstances.[20]

The Michigan reforms have been subject to a major evaluation study carried out by the University of Chicago.[21] The aims of the research were to describe procedures used to handle sexual assault cases in the criminal justice system and to examine the impact of the new statute. A major component of the research was the analysis of statistical crime data, but there were also intensive interviews with those responsible for the implementation of the new law. Changes in report, arrest and conviction rates which could be attributed to the new law were looked for, as were changes in the amount of discretion exercised by those in the criminal justice system, changes in the victim's experience and in the types of individuals protected by the law. Judges, prosecutors, defence attorneys, police officers and rape crisis centre staff were given structured interviews about their experience with sexual assault cases before and after the new law.

As far as statistical analyses of crime figures go, there was no significant difference in rape reports before and after law reform. There has been, however, a continuing increase over time which respondents in the study attributed to social change rather than to the specific effects of law reform, or to an absolute increase in the crime. The majority felt that a change in public attitudes towards rape was one of the most important influences on reporting trends. A significant finding was that arrests since law reform have been increasing at a faster rate than reports. Paradoxically, interviews with police and prosecutors reveal that there is still more doubt about victim credibility and false complaints for sexual assaults than there is for other violent crimes.

Most respondents attribute to the new law, and particularly to its provision prohibiting sexual history evidence, an increase in the rate of conviction as charged and a corresponding reduction in convictions for lesser offences. Others, however, feel that these changes were due to other innovations such as the increased clarity of the law and the degrees of sexual assault introduced by the new legislation.

The investigators were also interested in evaluating victims' experiences before and after reform and here the response was unequivocally positive. Over three-quarters of the respondents said that the victim's experience in the criminal justice system was less traumatic under the new law, and nearly half of these identified sexual history evidence prohibition as the most important factor in this.

The current trend in law reform

There is now overwhelming evidence to indicate that discretionary controls on the introduction of sexual history evidence are inadequate and unsatisfactory. As Berger has argued,

Lack of empathy and understanding manifested by judges presents the strongest counterargument against making the conservative, largely male judiciary primarily responsible for reforms. Moreover, shield laws not only serve to insulate the victim against irrational or biased rulings; they also aim to increase uniformity and hence predictability in practice. For these reasons one may favour specific provisions that leave little to the courts' predilections.[22]

Correspondingly, a number of jurisdictions seem to be moving towards provisions which leave little to the discretion of the judiciary. In addition to some American states, Canada introduced major changes to this effect in 1983. Nearer to home, the Scottish Law Commission's 1983 Report on evidence in rape cases goes some way, although not far enough, towards setting down guidelines regarding the admissibility of sexual history evidence. Nevertheless, the Scottish recommendations reflect a desire to move away from the absolute discretion which characterises English legislation:

we do not consider that the interests of justice can best be served by leaving with the judges a wholly unfettered discretion in such matters.[23]

One of the most frequently voiced objections to the introduction of something like total prohibition, even with a clear listing of exceptions, seems to be the perceived difficulty involved in drafting legislation. It has been argued, for example, that it is impossible to cater for all the possible situations which might arise in a rape trial and to anticipate all eventualities where various aspects of the victim's sexual experience might be relevant to the case. As the Scottish Law Commission explained this point,

the precise circumstances of each case in which a sexual offence is charged will differ, and it is impossible to predict with any certainty the kinds of circumstances which may arise in future cases. Moreover, items of evidence which in one case may be objectionable or irrelevant may be highly relevant in the circumstances of another.[24]

The problem of controlling sexual history evidence in rape cases has now been considered in great detail in England and elsewhere. Numerous reports and papers dealing with this issue in some depth in various common law jurisdictions have been published. There is also a fair amount of case law, as well as some evaluative research on the application of various legislative reforms. While reformers in the early 1970s undoubtedly had a difficult task on their hands, it can no longer be maintained with any credibility that we do not know enough to pass adequate legislation in this field. There is ample knowledge and experience to draw on in drafting legislation which, while minimising the role of discretion, could also deal adequately with the contingencies of rape cases that are likely to arise.

It must also be acknowledged that legislation alone, however strict, can have only a limited effect and is unlikely to solve all the problems involved in the social construction of rape that is manifest in and out of court. The process whereby the victim's character is under attack in rape trials is both complicated and subtle. As Newby comments,

in attempting to reinterpret events in favour of the defendant, counsel plays upon widely held sexual stereotypes and attitudes about appropriate female behaviour, to present the witness in a detrimental light. This is done through the employment of a combination of . . . various strategies, of which reference to the kinds of evidence precluded by special evidence laws, form only a small component.[25]

Nevertheless, it is crucial to get that small component right. In some jurisdictions at least, the lesson has been learnt. Here, it is widely assumed that the Sexual Offences (Amendment) Act 1976 has done all that is practicable to deal with this aspect of evidence in rape trials. Professor Honoré, for example, writes that the Act is

an important reform, which makes it clear that a woman is free to have sex outside marriage with Tom and Dick while refusing it to Harry and that her sex with Tom and Dick is no evidence that she consented to Harry's advances.[26]

That is certainly the spirit of the legislation, but in practice, as we have seen, the provisions of the 1976 Act fail adequately and uniformly to restrict evidence of her sexual activities with Tom and Dick. It is essential to ensure that the law works as the Heilbron group and Parliament originally intended. This will not happen so long as Section 2 remains entirely discretionary.

There is still great reluctance, particularly among members of the legal profession, to acknowledge that there is anything wrong with the operation of this part of the law. Unfortunately, the Criminal Law Revision Committee, whose report on the law relating to sexual offences was published in 1984, missed a golden opportunity of setting matters straight in this field.

The Criminal Law Revision Committee (CLRC) was asked, in consultation with the Policy Advisory Committee on Sexual Offences, to review the law relating to and penalties for sexual offences in July 1975. It was in the same month that the Heilbron Group was appointed to give urgent consideration to those aspects of rape law which were thought to be in need of immediate reform.

On the face of it, the CLRC appears to have accepted the model of law reform introduced by the Law Commission. The Commission's procedure is to publish a working paper which expounds the existing law, examines criticisms that have been directed at it and sets out the field of choice of reforms. Then follows the widest possible consultation with interested parties and, usually, the swift passage of a non-controversial Bill through Parliament. The CLRC started out by following this blueprint: they published a working paper in 1980 and invited comment on the provisional recommendations it contained. However, there the similarity between the workings of the two bodies ends. The final report published in 1984 strongly suggests that the CLRC has learnt little from the Law Commission with regard to rational procedures of law reform. Only in some areas does the final Report reflect the consultation that has taken place. In particular, representations by women's groups are dismissed in a perfunctory manner and the CLRC do not seem to be prepared to take seriously views with which they disagree.

Their approach to the working of the present law of rape is instructive. The Committee notes that television programmes and articles in the press and legal journals suggest that some people, in particular some women's organisations, think that complainants are inadequately protected because many judges too readily grant leave to cross-examine about sexual experience. At the time when the Report was written, the only empirical data about the working of the jurisdiction was part of the material reported in this book which had been published in a law journal. This evidence was dismissed in the Report in four sentences, as follows:

Critics do not seem to appreciate that a complainant's previous sexual experience may be relevant to the issue of consent. . . . The frequency with which leave is granted is no indication of the strength of the applications. Experienced advocates do not make applications unless they are reasonably sure that they will be granted. It is bad forensic practice to make applications which are likely to be refused.[27]

The first sentence is inaccurate. The other three are irrelevant to the conclusion reached from the findings of this study. The CLRC implicitly assume that there is general consensus about the concept of relevance. However, the operation of the law as well as common sense indicate that this is a misconception. The present state of affairs is bound to lead to uneven implementation and has important implications for the legal process.

Nevertheless, the Policy Advisory Committee and the CLRC, suspicious of independent data, decided to find out for themselves what the practice of the courts actually was. To this end, they

invited the Recorder of London to discuss this problem of giving leave to cross-examine with the circuit judges who sit regularly at the Central Criminal Court, because it had been suggested in the Press and in a television programme that leave to cross-examine had been given too freely at that court. The Policy Advisory Committee asked the Chairman of the Criminal Bar Association, who is now one of our members, to make enquiries amongst members of the Bar practising both in London and on the circuits as to the way Section 2 was applied.[28]

These investigations 'did not disclose any grounds for concern that either the letter or the spirit of section 2 of the 1976 Act was being disregarded. This is what we would have expected'.[29]

This is what anyone would have expected, given the type of enquiry which, the reader is bound to assume, was adopted to produce the result desired by the CLRC. What, one must ask, would the CLRC think of the confident finding that there was nothing to worry about by a Committee which sought to discover if public houses were habitually staying open after closing time by addressing inquiries as to whether the law was being properly observed to the Chairman of the Licensed Victuallers' Association and to the Brewers' Trade Association?

It has been impossible to secure uniformity in the exercise of the wide discretion inherent in Section 2. The present study shows that the law is being applied arbitrarily and unequally. There is now overwhelming evidence from this and other jurisdictions that broad discretionary schemes are, by definition, bound to fail. Elsewhere, legislation in the Section 2 mould has now been tightened up while here, the CLRC proposes to rely on judges to follow the rules in future, while acknowledging in passing that they may not have done so in the past. But the crux of the problem is that there are no clear rules and judges must in the end fall back on their own beliefs and values in making these decisions. It is unlikely that the will of Parliament will prevail when trial judges have totally unfettered discretion in such a controversial area, and when members of the CLRC, themselves largely senior members of the legal profession, assume that practitioners are the only reliable judges of how the law is working.

If legislative reform is to have any bite in this area, strong guidelines in accord with contemporary thinking and behaviour must replace the rag-bag of 'human experience in the courts' that currently governs the interpretation of the 1976 Act.

Chapter 10

An insoluble problem?

The treatment of rape victims by the law and the courts is grossly inadequate. It does little to help women to recover from the ordeal of rape and much to compound the initial trauma they experienced at the hands of the offender. This is partly due to legislative shortcomings and partly to the attitudes of members of the legal profession who administer the law. Those attitudes mirror broad societal myths and stereotypes about the nature of the offence and must be challenged as a matter of great urgency.

Despite a recognition of some of the main problems inherent in this area and legislative change in the mid-1970s, the court experience of the majority of rape victims remains virtually unchanged. The Sexual Offences (Amendment) Act 1976 has had little impact on the reporting, processing and trial of rape offences. Although their anonymity is by and large protected, women have not been encouraged to come forward and report rapes. The dominant flavour of rape trials has remained unchanged in spite of evidential restrictions. The practical application of the 1976 Act clearly flouts the intention of Parliament and, even more, the spirit of the Heilbron Report. The extension of the anonymity provision to defendants has created a serious anomaly which is still being questioned and, as argued in Chapter 4, should be done away with. Lastly, the decision in Morgan, which was said to be uncontroversial from a strictly legal point of view, has also remained a live issue.[1] It can no longer be assumed either that the 1976 provisions are non-problematic in themselves, or that they have been implemented properly.

This chapter considers the implications of these findings for future rape law, as well as for broader reforms which may be necessary if the offence of rape is to be cleansed of its present strongly anti-female bias, and if women are to build up any confidence in a system which in the past has been detrimental to their recovery from rape. In this context, the Report of the Criminal Law Revision Committee (CLRC) on Sexual Offences, which was published in 1984 and made a number of recommendations with regard to rape law, will also be considered.

The future of Section 2

This study establishes that there are striking differences among trial judges in their interpretation of the law and particularly in their willingness to exercise their discretion to exclude evidence of the victim's sexual biography. As we have seen, the majority of applications to introduce such evidence are successful. Most women who complain of rape are still subjected to distressing and irrelevant questioning about their intimate lives. Evidence from other sources confirms this. Rape Crisis Centre and Victim Support volunteers who frequently accompany women to court relate that such questioning is widespread, and the 1982 Chairman of the Bar Association was reported as saying that in his experience, 'Judges now always allowed that cross-examination to take place – always is too strong a word, but very frequently'.[2]

There is nothing novel in the English experience. The same problem has been encountered in a number of other jurisdictions, some of which, as we have seen, have moved away from discretionary schemes to stricter ways of controlling the admissibility of sexual history evidence.

It may be useful at this stage to recall the Heilbron Group's approach to this issue. That report forcefully and cogently argued that

in contemporary society sexual relationships outside marriage, both steady and of a more casual character, are fairly widespread, and it seems now to be agreed that a woman's sexual experiences with partners of her own choice are neither indicative of untruthfulness nor of a general willingness to consent. There exists, in our view, a gap between the assumptions underlying the law and those public views and attitudes which exist today which ought to influence today's law.[3]

This approach still has its critics. For example, Elliott, a professor of law, has argued that sexual history evidence is highly relevant in most instances, although perhaps not in cases involving a violent burglar or an assault by a complete stranger.[4] One of the main problems with this argument is that Elliott offers no justification for his contention that the victim's sexual history will 'shed much light' on the issues in the trial. Instead of making his assumptions explicit, he simply postulates that 'surely her sexual history is relevant' in a whole series of cases, relying on some dubious notion that if a woman has engaged in consensual sexual activity with someone, perhaps in slightly similar circumstances to the rape incident, this has substantial bearing on whether she consented to the defendant. In fact, it is difficult to see why her consent to sexual intercourse with others should be deemed to have any relevance to the likelihood of her consent to the defendant in question: after all, the identity of the partner is a crucial element in sexual intercourse and consent.

In any event, Parliament accepted several years ago now that in principle the Heilbron approach was right and made a commitment to its implementation by passing the Sexual Offences (Amendment) Act 1976. The important thing now is to ensure that the spirit of that legislation is adhered to in practice. In view of the evidence that Section 2 is not operating as intended, the time has come to give serious thought to replacing it with stronger legislation. One means of improving current practice would be to assist judges by laying down guiding principles: a clear indication of the circumstances in which a woman's sexual experience with A or B may be relevant to establish whether she was raped by C would undoubtedly help to remedy the worst problems which have arisen in applying the 1976 Act.

There had been some hint in 1982 that the case of R v Viola[5] might provide an opportunity for the Court of Appeal to establish some guidelines of this sort. The Court was told that the 1976 Act was operating well and had not worked unfairly against the defendant. While fairness to the defendant is one essential criterion for judging the success of legislative reform, it is clearly not the only criterion. There is more than a touch of irony in the conclusion that a law which was specifically designed to protect the complainant works well because it is not unfair to the defendant.

In any event, the case of Viola is not particularly helpful. It does little more than indulge in a semantic exercise by establishing that it is judgment, rather than discretion, that is involved in Section

2. This is of course correct to the extent that once the judge has decided that the proposed evidence has relevance to the case, he has no option but to allow it in as any other course of action would be unfair to the defendant. But the ruling begs the main question, which is how judges are to arrive at a sensible decision as to relevance. The Court of Appeal failed to explore or deal with the grey area between what is becoming increasingly obvious in this debate, namely that the distinction between the legal categories of credit and issue, where the issue is consent, is largely spurious as far as rape is concerned. As the situation stands now, judges will have to continue to rely on their own individual notions of the nature of rape and of appropriate female behaviour in interpreting this part of the law.

There is overwhelming evidence from this and other jurisdictions that schemes reliant on judicial discretion in controlling sexual history evidence are, by definition, bound to fail. Elsewhere, legislation in the Section 2 mould has now been tightened up while here the CLRC proposes to rely on judges to follow the rules in future, 'even if they have not done so in the past'.[6] But the crux of the problem is that there are no clear rules and judges must in the end fall back on their own beliefs and values in making these decisions. It is unlikely that the will of Parliament will prevail under the current law. If legislative reform is to be of any value in this area, strong guidelines in accord with contemporary thinking and behaviour must replace the essentially subjective decision-making that currently governs the interpretation of the 1976 Act.

The scope of rape law

According to the legal definition, a man commits rape if he has sexual intercourse with a woman without her consent, knowing that she does not consent or not caring one way or the other, provided he is over 14 years of age and not married to her. Sexual intercourse is confined to the penetration of the vagina by the penis – other forms of sexual penetration are excluded.

This narrow definition may be criticised on several grounds, the least controversial of which is the presumed impotence of boys under the age of 14. The absurdity of this proposition has finally been officially recognised, to the extent that the CLRC's 1984

Report on Sexual Offences recommended the elimination of this exemption from rape prosecution. We can only hope that the recommendation will be translated into legislative action in the very near future.

A far more controversial aspect of rape law is the exclusion of husbands from its ambit. The rationale for providing husbands with immunity from the charge of raping their wives is said to date from Hale's famous dictum to the effect that on marriage, the woman gives permanent and irretrievable consent to intercourse. Contemporary commentators have taken a different line. For example, Mitra has argued that by marrying, a woman

indicates no more than that she will usually consent to intercourse and it is fanciful in the extreme for the law to imply that by her vow she has deprived herself of the right to decline the act at any given time.[7]

In fact, since Hale, the courts have recognised that a wife can retract her consent in cases where there is some legally endorsed step towards separation or divorce. When a married couple are living apart without a court order, the law does not protect the woman from rape by her husband, although it has been established that the husband has no right to use force in obtaining intercourse. Another anomaly of the current position is that if a woman who is cohabiting without marriage is forced to have sexual intercourse by the man involved, his behaviour will come within the scope of the law of rape. Nevertheless, there is still wide divergence of opinion on the question of whether or not rape law should generally apply between spouses.

The opponents of reform feel that forced intercourse within marriage is not the 'grave and unique' offence that rape is outside marriage. It involves people who have had regular consensual intercourse in the past, which is believed to mitigate the gravity of the sexual aspect of the offence. Against that, it has been argued that a woman should be entitled to decide whether or not to have intercourse on any particular occasion and that her right to choose within marriage should be protected by the law.[8]

A second argument put forward against extending the law is that, because imprisonment would be unlikely in cases involving husbands and wives unless there were severe injuries, this might lead to all rape cases being regarded less seriously. Related to this is the argument that investigating the offence would be particularly difficult unless there was corroborating evidence, for example in the form of physical injury. Those in favour of reform say that the above arguments also apply to offence other than rape where they are committed within marriage, but have never been held to do so.

Problems of proof are considerable in any rape complaint, particularly where the issue is consent and where there is some relationship, however distant, between the parties involved before the alleged offence. In the present study there was not a single conviction without some corroborative evidence. Forensic evidence of sexual intercourse is generally of no probative value where the defence is consent. Recent complaint or evidence of distress, save in exceptional circumstances, do not amount to corroboration. Without injury or admissions by the accused, and preferably both, a conviction in any rape case is extremely unlikely. Nevertheless, it is clearly wrong for the law to condone criminal acts simply on the grounds that they are difficult to prove.

Third, it is argued that the creation of an offence of marital rape would be detrimental to the institution of marriage. Once a wife had made a complaint, she would be unable to withdraw it. Police intervention would drive the couple even further apart and lessen their chances of reconciliation which in turn would have detrimental consequences for the children. Whether reconciliation is always desirable is questionable: it is difficult to see whose interests would be served by the perpetuation of marriages where one partner severely abuses the other. But there are other offences too where prosecution of one member of the family is likely to have terminal consequences for family life – yet it has never been argued that father–daughter incest, for example, should be decriminalised because of this. The protection of the victim in that instance is given priority, rightly, over romantic notions regarding the sanctity of the family. Indeed, it makes far more sense to argue, as a minority of the CLRC have done, that police intervention

when the violence takes the form of forcible sexual intercourse may sometimes be in the wife's best interests and those of any children of the marriage.[9]

Finally, fear has been expressed that an offence of marital rape would be open to abuse by unscrupulous women, who may use a rape allegation as

a bargaining counter in negotiations for maintenance or custody, or as a basis of a charge of unreasonable behaviour in a divorce petition.[10]

Sufficiently unscrupulous wives are in fact able to use allegations of buggery in the same way under the current law, but, not surprisingly, such accusations against husbands are rarely made.

The CLRC, which considered the whole law relating to sexual offences in 1984, was in principle unequivocally opposed to the idea of according wives legal protection from rape. As they so eloquently put it,

if wives were to be treated in relation to rape in the same way as other women, that might lead to prosecutions which some would think were not desirable in the interest of the family or the public.[11]

Thus, their half-hearted recommendation was to extend the offence of rape to apply when the parties are effectively separated, whether with or without legal endorsement. Effective separation seems to refer to situations where there is no cohabitation and it is fully acknowledged that there may be considerable difficulties in defining cohabitation. If it proves impossible to find an adequate working definition, the majority would prefer to leave the law as it is rather than to extend it to all married couples.

It is undeniable that intercourse without consent can and does occur between spouses and the damage it inflicts can be just as devastating as any other rape. As one commentator put it, there is no evidence and no reason to assume that a woman suffers 'less pain, humiliation or fear from forcible sexual penetration by her husband, a boyfriend or a stranger'.[12]

The principle that non-consensual intercourse is a serious criminal offence, whoever its perpetrator or victim, must be endorsed by legislation as a matter of great urgency. It is unlikely that a change in the law to cover all married couples would precipitate vast numbers of complaints by wives against husbands. Certainly this has not been the experience of other jurisdictions where the marital immunity from rape prosecution has, to varying degrees, been repealed. While the immediate practical impact of such law reform may be minimal, it would go a long way towards establishing the principle of freedom of sexual choice within marriage and some measure of equality between husbands and wives. And, as Williams comments,

The primary purpose of the criminal law should not be to secure the maximum number of convictions, rather it is to educate people as to standards of behaviour which society expects of them.[13]

The second major criticism of the legal definition of rape is that it is confined to sexual intercourse and excludes other forms of sexual penetration. It may well be that the only factor that distinguishes rape from indecent assault is the object of penetration and there is no logic in keeping as totally separate the treatment by the law of offences which are all on a continuum of sexual violence committed by men against women. There are certainly strong arguments to include within the ambit of rape law such acts as non-consensual oral intercourse, anal intercourse (whether on a man or woman) and any form of vaginal penetration. However, there has been a certain degree of reluctance to extend the definition in this way, on two main grounds discussed by the CLRC. The first of these is that the concept of rape is 'well established in popular thought and corresponds to a distinctive form of wrong-doing'.[14]

There are indications, however, that this assumption is not justified. Card, for example, has noted that the concept of rape is now popularly understood to include behaviour other than that covered by the legal definition. He cites as an illustration the frequent use of terms such as 'oral rape' and 'homosexual rape' in the press.[15] Further support for his view comes from the case of Rai,[16] a man who received a partly suspended sentence for the rape of a girl of 6. When the transcript of the case became available, it turned out that the judge in fact sentenced Rai for indecent assault because he did not technically achieve penetration. The niceties of this legal distinction were probably lost on the general public and indeed on the press, which continued to be outraged by the leniency of the sentence despite this new piece of information. One may well speculate that many people would be surprised to learn just how limited the legal definition of rape is.

Second, it has been argued that the risk of pregnancy is a unique characteristic of rape and that this too sets it apart from other forms of non-consensual sexual activity. This really is a spurious argument, for several reasons. First, although the risk of pregnancy is much reduced, it cannot be excluded in anal intercourse. Second, the prevention of unwanted pregnancy is obviously not a major reason for criminalising rape. As Temkin has argued,

the fact that pre-pubertal, menopausal, sterilised and infertile women as well as those who practice contraception are all covered by the law of rape suggests that this distinction is not of overriding significance.[17]

An important feature of rape law reform in the USA and some Australian states has been the broadening of the legal definition of rape so that it is not limited to sexual intercourse but covers a range of coercive sexual acts. The trend has been towards such reform after experimenting with minor procedural alterations in rules of evidence, not unlike Section 2 of the 1976 Act in England. A number of commentators would like to see a similar trend in this country. The National Council for Civil Liberties, for example, believes that rape law should be widened to include other forms of sexual penetration and serious sexual assault.[18] Card has also argued that the CLRC was wrong not to propose the merging of various types of non-consensual sexual penetration into a single offence, which would serve the dual purpose of simplifying the law and bringing it in line with popular opinion.

There are two major problems which could lead to injustice under the present situation. First, the maximum penalty for indecent assault is currently ten years. This is a great improvement on the pre-1985 situation where this offence was punishable by a maximum of two years when committed against a female and ten years when committed against a male. However, it is questionable whether even the new maximum penalty is, as it was intended, adequate to deal with the worst cases. The new maximum penalty implies that the worst indecent assault can never be as severe as the worst rape – yet attempted rape now carries a maximum penalty of life imprisonment. There is clearly no significant difference between one sort of non-consensual sexual penetration and another and no logic in fixing the maximum penalty at life for one and at ten years for the other.

An insoluble problem?

The second important injustice which arises from the current distinction between the legal categories of rape, indecent assault and buggery is that the various provisions which apply to protect victims of rape under the Sexual Offences (Amendment) Act 1976 do not apply to these related offences. There is no equivalent to Section 2 to safeguard them from cross-exanination as to their sexual experience to show that they were likely to consent to the incident which constitutes the subject matter of the charge. This means that a victim in a case of buggery or indecent assault can be freely questioned about her previous sexual experience, without defence counsel having to show the relevance of his cross-examination to the case. In a case included in the present study, a man was charged with several counts of buggery and indecent assault, as well as with one count of rape on the same woman. Defence counsel began by questioning her as to her past experience of buggery and eventually made an application under Section 2 in respect of the rape charge. In giving him leave for further cross-examination, the judge wryly remarked that 'it was only the existence of the rape count which posed the difficulty'.

The CLRC's final Report aims to remedy this situation and to bring in line the law relating to rape and indecent assault. It recommends that Section 2 of the Sexual Offences (Amendment) Act 1976 should be extended to cover cases of indecent assault. Notwithstanding the criticisms made of the operation of Section 2, this is a welcome and logical recommendation which is in need of urgent implementation.

However, the CLRC has not gone far enough in putting rape on a par with other offences involving sexual penetration. The above argument goes for extending the anonymity provision accorded to rape victims in the 1976 Act to victims of indecent assault and buggery. It is no less distressing for a victim of non-consensual sexual penetration than for a victim of rape to have personal details published in the local press.

Whether acts of non-consensual oral intercourse or vaginal penetration by various objects are included within the legal category of rape is probably not the main issue. What is of crucial importance, however, is that the gravity of these behaviours should be fully recognised by the law and that the protection extended to victims of rape is also extended to victims of other forms of non-consensual sexual acts.

An insoluble problem?

Corroboration

Another antiquated and blatantly sexist element in the law of rape is the practice of warning juries of the danger of convicting on the victim's evidence alone. Although it is still widely believed that rape is an offence particularly prone to false complaints, there is no evidence to substantiate this. Despite serious challenge, the law continues to require judges to warn juries against the dangers of convicting on the woman's uncorroborated evidence. 'Human experience in the courts' and 'long judicial experience' are said to conform with Hale's view and to justify continuation of this practice.

The CLRC's final Report does not discuss the question of corroboration. Presumably, it was felt to have been adequately dealt with in the past. While their Working Paper recognises that it may be 'offensive' for a rape victim to hear the judge directing the jury as to corroboration, it remains firm in the position it had adopted by a majority in its 1972 Report on Evidence that special caution is needed in sexual cases because, it is said,

women and girls ... sometimes allege that they have been raped in order to explain away evidence leading to the inference that they have recently had sexual intercourse.[19]

There are already more than adequate safeguards to counter the effect of possible false complaints in the criminal law in general (e.g. cross-examination of the victim, defence speech to the jury, threat of prosecution for perjury) and in rape in particular where the barriers to successful prosecution are known to be enormous from deterrents early on in the system (police questioning, medical examination) and right through to the trial stage where cross-examination is far wider in scope than in other trials. There is no logic in arguing that, in such circumstances, the corroboration warning is needed as a safeguard against false complaints in sexual offences.

It is not always appreciated that judges often make comments in the guise of a corroboration warning to the jury which are nothing less than a fundamental insult to women. The following extracts are taken from trials in this study to provide some illustrations:

An insoluble problem?

Experience has shown that it is very dangerous to convict a man of an offence of this nature on the unsupported evidence of a woman. These offences are very easy to allege – some people may have strange motives and reasons for alleging them, the imagination can play tricks. It is dangerous to convict on the evidence of the complainant alone. For this reason, it has become a healthy practice in law to warn juries about that.

It is easy to make an allegation of rape: only the girl and the man are present – how on earth is the man to disprove it? Women do make false accusations out of fantasy or spite. That's why doctors always have a nurse present. Juries are warned that they shouldn't convict if they're not aware of this. They should look for corroboration, for example, doctor's evidence of injury or admissions to the police.

The experience of these courts is that sometimes women make up such charges – I ask you to accept that. It is dangerous to convict in a sexual case on the word of a woman.

In sex cases, whatever the sex of the complainant, it is dangerous to convict on the girl's [sic] evidence unless there is corroboration of it against the defendant.

These extracts show how the corroboration warning can serve to reinforce for the jury the stereotype of the malicious, vindictive and sometimes unbalanced rape victim which pervades the legal system. As the New South Wales Attorney General commented in introducing sexual assault law reforms there,

It is stressed that the present practice [of corroboration warning] is regarded as being grossly offensive to women, and discriminatory. ... Under Section 405C the judge will not be compelled to utilize the traditional formula of denigration which identifies women as especially untrustworthy.[20]

One function of the law should be to challenge assumptions about culturally acceptable behaviour towards women and thus contribute to more enlightened attitudes towards the offence. It is regrettable that the CLRC's final Report missed the opportunity to recommend long overdue change in this area. As with marital rape, the effect of repealing the corroboration requirement may have little practical impact. Nevertheless, a matter of principle is at stake. If the law is to be widely respected by women, it is essential that it should get rid of its inherited view of the rape victim as a neurotic female, particularly prone to lying and to sexual hysteria. One crucial step would be to drop the practice of a judicial warning about the danger of accepting the victim's uncorroborated evidence that gives a ritual public reinforcement of this image at every rape trial.

Matters of procedure

If a major policy objective in this area is to encourage more victims to come forward and report rape and to sustain the complaint through to trial, considerable efforts must be made to render the criminal justice system more sensitive to their needs and to ensure that their court experience is as painless and dignified as possible. In addition to the substantive reforms outlined above, a number of procedural innovations would contribute to this goal without in any way detracting from the rights of the defendant.

One major grievance of rape victims is the uncertainty over the dates of the trial. Under the current system, as we have seen there may be very lengthy delays in bringing a defendant to trial and the trial dates may be changed several times. For the victim, this can mean attending court when the case is first listed, possibly at very short notice, waiting for a whole day, only to be told that the trial is being rescheduled for some other time. This cannot fail to add to her anxiety about the whole process and may explain in part why some victims are ultimately so reluctant to give evidence. There is no good reason why dates for rape trials could not be fixed in advance and adhered to. This would undoubtedly go some way towards giving the victim some feeling of control and security at a time when these are essential to her swift recovery from the trauma of rape.

Another source of distress for the rape victim is her unwanted proximity to the defendant and his family and friends while she is waiting to go into court and give evidence. The waiting period may be lengthy, which gives her quite enough to contend with. An encounter with the assailant, or exposure to his family's conversations about their view of the offence or of her reputation, are bound to provoke considerable anxiety, embarrassment and humiliation in the victim. This can easily be avoided by the provision of a safe waiting area for rape victims during the proceedings.

Once in court, the victim's anonymity should be ensured. If her name and/or address are not already known to the defendant, there is no justification whatsoever for disclosing these to him during the course of the trial. While some judges insist that the victim is not referred to by her full name during the trial, this practice is far from universal. Since there is a legislative commitment to preserving the rape victim's anonymity in press reports, there can be no argument for inconsistency when it comes to court proceedings, where she is in effect exposed to publicity which is far more direct and potentially just as damaging as if she were named in a local newspaper.

This book has drawn attention to the victim's ordeal in giving evidence at a rape trial. A substantial tightening of sexual history legislation would lessen this, but it would of course not affect some parts of the evidence she is required to produce. For example, she would still have to describe the sexual elements of the offence in considerable detail. One way of making this less onerous would be to give the victim the right to give her evidence in as much privacy as possible within the confines of court procedure. Judges already have discretion to hear evidence in camera if they deem this to be necessary, for example in cases involving child witnesses. There is no reason why victims of serious sexual assaults should not have a right to be protected in the same way. The certainty that they will not have to recount the whole story to a public gallery filled with the defendant's entourage, their own neighbours or colleagues or indeed perfect strangers who are there out of mere curiosity, should do much to allay their anxieties about the whole trial process.

Finally, it must be recognised that rape victims need some degree of support during their time in court. They may choose to rely on a member of their family, a friend or on more formal contacts such as Rape Crisis Centre workers or victim support volunteers. Victims should have a right to have someone of their choice sitting in the well of the court while they are giving evidence. The support they may derive from the presence of a sympathetic outsider at such an exceptionally stressful time is clearly very valuable indeed. Under the current system, where the matter is dependent on the sympathies of the trial judge, volunteers from victim support organisations have occasionally found themselves in the witness box being questioned and cross-examined about the nature of their role and relationship with the victim. The right to have such a person present must not be capable of being challenged.

These suggestions for procedural reform are not intended to be exhaustive, but rather to point to areas where with relatively little effort and without detriment to the accused, the victim's ordeal in court could be lessened to a considerable degree. Further research into the experience of rape victims in the criminal justice system is badly needed and would undoubtedly identify other areas where procedural change would be beneficial in minimising the trauma inherent in such a court appearance.

But we must go beyond legislative and procedural change if there is to be a real improvement in the treatment of rape victims by the legal institutions. As we have seen, the role of the judiciary and of members of the bar is crucial in the implementation of both substantive law and court procedure. Currently, they are ill-equipped to do this effectively. The National Council for Civil Liberties has documented that our predominantly middle-class, middle-aged male judges 'often express stereotype notions about women and show little understanding of the nature of women's lives'.[21] Increased understanding in this area is vital and the suggestion has been made that training on the impact of the law and the legal system might counteract the current stereotypical views held by the judiciary which so clearly govern the trial of rape offences. Barristers and law students would also benefit from similar training, which should help them to become aware of stereotyped attitudes to women.

Conclusion

When the CLRC produced its final Report in 1984, the media showed some optimism that its recommendations would be followed by legislative reform. Unfortunately, however, even if the political climate were favourable to change, the proposals contained in the CLRC's Report are insufficient to bring rape law into line with contemporary needs, attitudes and behaviour. An interesting aside is that there is a marked contrast between the tone and approach of the CLRC and of the Advisory Group on the Law of Rape towards the plight of the rape victim. One wonders to what extent this is explained by the composition of the two committees. Only two of the seventeen members of the CLRC, drawn mainly from the legal profession, were women. The membership of the Advisory Group on the Law of Rape, on the other hand, was more evenly divided between the sexes and was also chaired by a woman. It also produced a more sympathetic, balanced and sensitive report than the CLRC.

There is considerable ambiguity in society and in the legal system towards the plight of the rape victim. On the one hand, there has been growing awareness since the mid-1970s that rape victims are getting a rough deal from the various institutions they come into contact with when they report the offence. Measures like the Sexual Offences (Amendment) Act 1976 have gone some way towards attempting to remedy this situation. On the other hand, there is convincing evidence that legislative reform has not gone far enough. Not only is the scope of the Act very limited, but each of its provisions designed to help the victim is matched with a provision to favour the defendant. Furthermore, the essentially discretionary nature of the legislation, a male judiciary and a conservative criminal bar have meant that its practical impact has been minimal. During the debates of the Bill, one MP opposed to it expressed his hope that judges would 'have sufficient ingenuity to whittle it down'.[22] The findings of this study suggest that his hopes were not misplaced.

If we are to have a rape law that meets the essential need of being fair to the defendant but also affords adequate protection for the victim, which is essential if our society is not to decriminalise the offence by continuing to discourage the reporting of rape, some vital changes are urgently required. The first priority must be to ensure that the Sexual Offences (Amendment) Act 1976 works as intended by Parliament and this involves the strengthening of Section 2. Anonymity for defendants, which was introduced to pacify those who felt that anonymity for complainants alone would give rise to an upsurge in malicious accusations and which has had certain unforeseen and unfortunate consequences, should be repealed as the CLRC's Fifteenth Report recommends. The Morgan decision which, in the light of subsequent case law, has turned out to be more controversial than was first presumed, should also be reconsidered with regard to its application to rape.

In addition to strengthening the 1976 Act, a number of other reforms are urgently needed. The gravity of other forms of non-consensual sexual penetration and contact must be recognised by the law. As has been argued, victims of indecent assault should also be entitled to the same protection vis-à-vis their sexual history and anonymity as victims of rape. Husbands should be brought within the compass of rape law and it is high time to get rid of the anachronistic assumption that on marriage women relinquish their right to refuse sexual intercourse. Finally, the corroboration requirement which serves to perpetuate the myth that women are particularly untrustworthy witnesses and prone to lying on oath should be repealed. It is also important that future reforms leave as little as possible to judicial discretion. A number of relatively minor procedural reforms designed to lighten the ordeal women currently experience when they appear in court to give evidence in a rape case should also be introduced. Finally, priority must be given to training members of the legal profession in this area and to develop among them attitudes which are conducive to the effective implementation of the law.

Further research in this area is also of crucial importance. Both the Advisory Group on the Law of Rape and the CLRC have clearly been greatly hampered in their work by the fact that so little reliable information exists in this country about the nature of the offence, its effect on victims, the motivations of offenders and the role of societal institutions in compounding its impact on victims. Both bodies have had to rely almost exclusively on assumptions and empirical data predominantly from the USA regarding various aspects of the problem. Unfortunately, the CLRC's 1984 Report gives little confidence that it would use empirical data if it had them or that it would be capable of distinguishing reliable from unreliable data.

A 1981 Law Commission Report on divorce and maintenance recommends that provision be made for the continuous monitoring of legislation dealing with the financial consequences of divorce. A similar case could well be made out for setting up machinery for the systematic monitoring of the law relating to rape, partly to identify potential areas for future reform and partly to ensure that the operation of current legislation is in line with the intentions of Parliament.

Finally, it must be remembered that law reform, however comprehensive and well implemented, is only part of the solution.

An insoluble problem?

There are clearly limits to how much can be achieved by procedural change. In an adversarial system some attack on the chief prosecution witness's evidence is standard strategy and any defence lawyer will capitalise on information which, however prejudicial from the victim's point of view, is in favour of his client. As Wood has argued from American experience,

Temporary measures, such as crisis centres or legislative reforms, may be able to alleviate current atrocities, but until the time when the rape victim is no longer looked upon with suspicion and distrust, most rapists are likely to commit the crime with impunity. The bias against the rape victim ... can only be dispelled if people become aware of the quandary in which she has been placed by a society which tends to adopt a male perspective. Exposing the defects in the present system is the first step in curing them.[23]

The present position of the rape victim is partly the result of legal definitions of rape and of an essential and proper concern to afford maximum protection for accused persons in an adversarial system. But the legal system is an integral part of society and subject to the same values. Thus, the experience of rape victims in court is also a product of current social attitudes towards sexuality and the 'proper' nature of male and female relationships.

The ambivalence towards the rape victim which has characterised both the substance and the application of the Sexual Offences (Amendment) Act 1976 has to be resolved without further delay if this area of the criminal law is to recover credibility. It is imperative to get away from the attitudes embodied in the current legal process, attitudes which are not only insulting and degrading to women, but which also hamper the administration of justice in the broadest sense of the term.

Appendix

The Sexual Offences (Amendment) Act 1976

1976 Chapter 82

An Act to amend the law relating to rape [22nd November, 1976]

Be it enacted by the Queen's most Excellent Majesty, by and with the advice and consent of the Lords Spiritual and Temporal, and Commons, in this present Parliament assembled, and by the authority of the same, as follows:

1. – (1) For the purposes of section 1 of the Sexual Offences Act 1956 (which relates to rape) a man commits rape if –
    (a) he has unlawful sexual intercourse with a woman who at the time of the intercourse does not consent to it; and
    (b) at that time he knows that she does not consent to the intercourse or he is reckless as to whether she consents to it; and references to rape in other enactments (including the following provisions of this Act) shall be construed accordingly.

    (2) It is hereby declared that if at a trial for a rape offence the jury has to consider whether a man believed that a woman was consenting to sexual intercourse, the presence or absence of reasonable grounds for such a belief is a matter to which the jury is to have regard, in conjunction with any other relevant matters, in considering whether he so believed.

2. – (1) If at a trial any person is for the time being charged with a rape offence to which he pleads not guilty, then, except with the

leave of the judge, no evidence and no question in cross-examination shall be adduced or asked at the trial, by or on behalf of any defendant at the trial, about any sexual experience of a complainant with a person other than that defendant.

(2) The judge shall not give leave in pursuance of the preceding subsection for any evidence or question except on an application made to him in the absence of the jury by or on behalf of a defendant; and on such an application the judge shall give leave if and only if he is satisfied that it would be unfair to that defendant to refuse to allow the evidence to be adduced or the question to be asked.

(3) In subsection (1) of this section 'complainant' means a woman upon whom, in a charge for a rape offence to which the trial in question relates, it is alleged that rape was committed, attempted or proposed.

(4) Nothing in this section authorises evidence to be adduced or a question to be asked which cannot be adduced or asked apart from this section.

3. – (1) Where a magistrates' court inquires into a rape offence as examining justices, then, except with the consent of the court, evidence shall not be adduced and a question shall not be asked at the inquiry which, if the inquiry were a trial at which a person is charged as mentioned in subsection (1) of the preceding section and each of the accused at the inquiry were charged at the trial with the offences of which he is accused at the inquiry, could not be adduced or asked without leave in pursuance of that section.

(2) On an application for consent in pursuance of the preceding subsection for any evidence or question the court shall –
(a) refuse the consent unless the court is satisfied that leave in respect of the evidence or question would be likely to be given at a relevant trial; and
(b) give the consent if the court is so satisfied.

(3) Where a person charged with a rape offence is tried for that offence either by court-martial or summarily before a magistrates' court in pursuance of section 6(1) of the Children and Young Persons Act 1969 (which provides for the summary trial in certain

cases of persons under the age of 17 who are charged with indictable offences) the preceding section shall have effect in relation to the trial as if –

    (a) the words 'in the absence of the jury' in subsection (2) were omitted; and

    (b) for any reference to the judge there were substituted –

        (i) in the case of a trial by court-martial for which a judge advocate is appointed, a reference to the judge advocate, and

        (ii) in any other case, a reference to the court.

4. – (1) Subject to subsection (7)(a) of this section, after a person is accused of a rape offence no matter likely to lead members of the public to identify a woman as the complainant in relation to that accusation shall either be published in England and Wales in a written publication available to the public or be broadcast in England and Wales except as authorised by a direction given in pursuance of this section.

(2) If, before the commencement of a trial at which a person is charged with a rape offence, he or another person against whom the complainant may be expected to give evidence at the trial applies to a judge of the Crown Court for a direction in pursuance of this subsection and satisfies the judge –

    (a) that the direction is required for the purpose of inducing persons to come forward who are likely to be needed as witnesses at the trial; and

    (b) that the conduct of the applicant's defence at the trial is likely to be substantially prejudiced if the direction is not given, the judge shall direct that the preceding subsection shall not, by virtue of the accusation alleging the offence aforesaid, apply in relation to the complainant.

(3) If at a trial before the Crown Court at which a person is charged with a rape offence the judge is satisfied that the effect of subsection (1) of this section is to impose a substantial and unreasonable restriction upon the reporting of proceedings at the trial and that it is in the public interest to remove or relax the restriction, he shall direct that that subsection shall not apply to such matter relating to the complainant as is specified in the

direction; but a direction shall not be given in pursuance of this subsection by reason only of an acquittal of a defendant at the trial.

(4) If a person who has been convicted of an offence and given notice of appeal to the Court of Appeal against the conviction, or notice of an application for leave so to appeal, applies to the Court of Appeal for a direction in pursuance of this subsection and satisfies the Court –

(a) that the direction is required for the purpose of obtaining evidence in support of the appeal; and

(b) that the applicant is likely to suffer substantial injustice if the direction is not given,

the Court shall direct that subsection (1) of this section shall not, by virtue of an accusation which alleges a rape offence and is specified in the direction, apply in relation to a complainant so specified.

(5) If any matter is published or broadcast in contravention of subsection (1) of this section, the following persons, namely –

(a) in the case of a publication in a newspaper or periodical, any proprietor, any editor and any publisher of the newspaper or periodical;

(b) in the case of any other publication, the person who publishes it; and

(c) in the case of a broadcast, any body corporate which transmits or provides the programme in which the broadcast is made and any person having functions in relation to the programme corresponding to those of an editor of a newspaper,

shall be guilty of an offence and liable on summary conviction to a fine not exceeding £500.

(6) For the purposes of this section a person is accused of a rape offence if –

(a) an information is laid alleging that he has committed a rape offence; or

(b) he appears before a court charged with a rape offence; or

(c) a court before which he is appearing commits him for trial on a new charge alleging a rape offence; or

(d) a bill of indictment charging him with a rape offence is preferred before a court in which he may lawfully be indicted for the offence, and references in this section and section 7(5) of this Act to an accusation alleging a rape offence shall be construed accordingly; and in this section –

'a broadcast' means a broadcast by wireless telegraphy of sound or visual images intended for general reception, and cognate expressions shall be construed accordingly;

'complainant', in relation to a person accused of a rape offence or an accusation alleging a rape offence, means the woman against whom the offence is alleged to have been committed; and

'written publication' includes a film, a sound track and any other record in permanent form but does not include an indictment or other document prepared for use in particular legal proceedings.

(7) Nothing in this section –

(a) prohibits the publication or broadcasting, in consequence of an accusation alleging a rape offence, of matter consisting only of a report of legal proceedings other than proceedings at, or intended to lead to, or on an appeal arising out of, a trial at which the accused is charged with that offence; or

(b) affects any prohibition or restriction imposed by virtue of any other enactment upon a publication or broadcast;

and a direction in pursuance of this section does not affect the operation of subsection (1) of this section at any time before the direction is given.

5. – (1) In relation to a person charged with a rape offence in pursuance of any provision of the Naval Discipline Act 1957, the Army Act 1955 or the Air Force Act 1955, the preceding section shall have effect with the following modifications, namely –

(a) any reference to a trial or a trial before the Crown Court shall be construed as a reference to a trial by court-martial;

(b) in subsection (1) after the word 'Wales' in both places there shall be inserted the words 'or Northern Ireland';

(c) for any reference in subsection (2) to a judge of the Crown Court there shall be substituted a reference to the officer who is authorised to convene or has convened a court-martial for the trial of the offence (or, if after convening it he has ceased to hold the appointment by virtue of which he convened it, the officer holding that appointment) and for any reference in subsection (3) to such a judge there shall be substituted a reference to the court;

(d) for any reference in subsection (4) to the Court of Appeal there shall be substituted a reference to the Courts-Martial Appeal Court; and

(e) in subsection (6) for paragraphs (a) to (d) there shall be substituted the words 'he is charged with a rape offence in pursuance of any provision of the Naval Discipline Act 1957, the Army Act 1955 or the Air Force Act 1955'.

(2) If after the commencement of a trial at which a person is charged with a rape offence a new trial of the person for that offence is ordered, the commencement of any previous trial at which he was charged with that offence shall be disregarded for the purposes of subsection (2) of the preceding section.

(3) In relation to a conviction of an offence tried summarily as mentioned in section 3(3) of this Act, for references to the Court of Appeal in subsection (4) of the preceding section there shall be substituted references to the Crown Court and the reference to notice of an application for leave to appeal shall be omitted.

(4) When an offence under subsection (5) of the preceding section which has been committed by a body corporate is proved to have been committed with the consent or connivance of, or to be attributable to any neglect on the part of, any director, manager, secretary or other similar officer of the body corporate or any person who was purporting to act in any such capacity, he as well as the body corporate shall be guilty of that offence and be liable to be proceeded against and punished accordingly.

Where the affairs of a body corporate are managed by its members the preceding provisions of this subsection shall apply in relation to the acts and defaults of a member in connection with his functions of management as if he were a director of the body corporate.

(5) Proceedings for an offence under subsection (5) of the preceding section (including such an offence which is alleged to have been committed by virtue of the preceding subsection) shall not be instituted except by or with the consent of the Attorney General or, if the offence is alleged to have been committed in Northern Ireland, of the Attorney General for Northern Ireland; and where a person is charged with such an offence it shall be a defence to

prove that at the time of the alleged offence he was not aware, and neither suspected nor had reason to suspect, that the publication or broadcast in question was of such matter as is mentioned in subsection (1) of that section.

(6) In section 31(1) of the Criminal Appeal Act 1968 (which provides that certain powers of the Court of Appeal may be exercised by a single judge) after the word '1973' there shall be inserted the words 'and the power to give directions under section 4(4) of the Sexual Offences (Amendment) Act 1976'; and in section 36(1) of the Courts-Martial (Appeals) Act 1968 (which provides that certain powers of the Courts-Martial Appeal Court may be exercised by a single judge) after paragraph (g) there shall be inserted the words 'and the power to give directions under section 4(4) of the Sexual Offences (Amendment) Act 1976 as adapted by section 5(1)(d) of that Act'.

6. – (1) After a person is accused of a rape offence no matter likely to lead members of the public to identify him as the person against whom the accusation is made shall either be published in England and Wales in a written publication available to the public or be broadcast in England and Wales except –

(a) as authorised by a direction given in pursuance of this section or by section 4(7)(a) of this Act as applied by subsection (6) of this section; or

(b) after he has been convicted of the offence at a trial before the Crown Court.

(2) If a person accused of a rape offence applies to a magistrates' court, before the commencement of his trial for that offence, for a direction in pursuance of this subsection, the court shall direct that the preceding subsection shall not apply to him in consequence of the accusation; and if at a trial before the Crown Court at which a person is charged with a rape offence in respect of which he has not obtained such a direction –

(a) the judge is satisfied that the effect of the preceding subsection is to impose a substantial and unreasonable restriction on the reporting of proceedings at the trial and that it is in the public interest to remove the restriction in respect of that person; or

(b) that person applies to the judge for a direction in pursuance

of this subsection,
the judge shall direct that the preceding subsection shall not apply
to that person in consequence of the accusation alleging that
offence.

(3) If, before the commencement of a trial at which a person is
charged with a rape offence, another person who is to be charged
with a rape offence at the trial applies to a judge of the Crown
Court for a direction in pursuance of this subsection and satisfies
the judge –
(a) that the direction is required for the purpose of inducing
persons to come forward who are likely to be needed as witnesses
at the trial; and
(b) that the conduct of the applicant's defence at the trial is
likely to be substantially prejudiced if the direction is not given,
the judge shall direct that subsection (1) of this section shall not,
by virtue of the accusation alleging the offence with which the
first-mentioned person is charged, apply to him.

(4) In relation to a person charged with a rape offence in
pursuance of any provision of the Naval Discipline Act 1957, the
Army Act 1955 or the Air Force Act 1955, the preceding provisions
of this section shall have effect with the following modifications,
namely –
(a) any reference to a trial or a trial before the Crown Court
shall be construed as a reference to a trial by court-martial;
(b) after the word 'Wales' in both places there shall be inserted
the words 'or Northern Ireland';
(c) in subsection (2) for any reference to a judge of the Crown
Court there shall be substituted a reference to the court-martial;
and
(d) in subsection (2) for any reference to a magistrates' court
and in subsection (3) for any reference to a judge of the Crown
Court there shall be substituted a reference to the officer who is
authorised to convene or has convened a court-martial for the
trial of the offence or, if after convening it he has ceased to hold
the appointment by virtue of which he convened it, the officer
holding that appointment.

(5) An order in pursuance of section 49 of the Children and
Young Persons Act 1933 (which among other things imposes

restrictions on reports of certain court proceedings concerning juveniles but authorises the court and the Secretary of State to make orders lifting the restrictions for the purpose of avoiding injustice to a juvenile) may include a direction that subsection (1) of this section shall not apply to a person in respect of whom the order is made.

(6) Subsections (5) to (7) of section 4 of this Act shall have effect for the purposes of this section as if for references to that section there were substituted references to this section; and –

(a) in relation to a person charged as mentioned in subsection (4) of this section, section 4(6) of this Act, as applied by this subsection, shall have effect as if for paragraphs (a) to (d) there were substituted the words 'he is charged with a rape offence in pursuance of any provision of the Naval Discipline Act 1957, the Army Act 1955 or the Air Force Act 1955';

(b) in section 5(2) of this Act the reference to the purposes of section 4(2) of this Act shall be construed as including a reference to the purposes of subsections (2) and (3) of this section; and

(c) in relation to a person charged by virtue of this subsection with such an offence as is mentioned in subsection (5) of section 5 of this Act, that subsection shall have effect as if for the reference to section 4(1) of this Act there were substituted a reference to subsection (1) of this section.

7. – (1) This Act may be cited as the Sexual Offences (Amendment) Act 1976, and this Act and the Sexual Offences Acts 1956 and 1967 may be cited together as the Sexual Offences Acts 1956 to 1976.

(2) In this Act –

'a rape offence' means any of the following, namely rape, attempted rape, aiding, abetting, counselling and procuring rape or attempted rape, and incitement to rape; and

references to sexual intercourse shall be construed in accordance with section 44 of the Sexual Offences Act 1956 so far as it relates to natural intercourse (under which such intercourse is deemed complete on proof of penetration only);

and section 46 of that Act (which relates to the meaning of 'man' and 'woman' in that Act) shall have effect as if the reference to that Act included a reference to this Act.

(3) In relation to such a trial as is mentioned in subsection (2) of section 1 of this Act which is a trial by court-martial or a summary trial by a magistrates' court, references to the jury in that subsection shall be construed as references to the court.

(4) This Act shall come into force on the expiration of the period of one month beginning with the date on which it is passed, except that sections 5(1)(b) and 6(4)(b) shall come into force on such day as the Secretary of State may appoint by order made by by statutory instrument.

(5) Sections 2 and 3 of this Act shall not have effect in relation to a trial or inquiry which begins before the expiration of that period and sections 4 and 6 of this Act shall not have effect in relation to an accusation alleging a rape offence which is made before the expiration of that period.

(6) This Act, except so far as it relates to courts-martial and the Courts-Martial Appeal Court, shall not extend to Scotland and this Act, except so far as it relates to courts-martial and the Courts-Martial Appeal Court (including such a publication or broadcast in Northern Ireland as is mentioned in section 4(1) as adapted by section 5(1)(b) and section 6(1) as adapted by section 6(4)(b), shall not extend to Northern Ireland.

Notes

1 The trouble with rape

1 DPP v Morgan and others (1975), 61 Cr.App.R. 136.
2 *Report of the Advisory Group on the Law of Rape*, London, HMSO, 1975.
3 See full text in Appendix.
4 *Daily Telegraph*, 7 January 1982.
5 R v Roberts and Roberts (1982), 4 Cr.App.R. (S).
6 *Guardian*, 16 December 1982.
7 *New Law Journal*, 4 November 1982.
8 Griffin, S.: 'Rape – the all-American crime', *Ramparts*, vol. 10, no. 3, 1971; Horos, C. V.: *Rape*, New Canaan, Tobey Publishing Co, 1974; Brownmiller, S.: *Against Our Will: Men, Women and Rape*, London, Secker and Warburg, 1975.
9 Rape Counselling and Research Project: *Third Report*, London 1982.
10 Unpublished research findings, Department of Social Policy and Social Science, Royal Holloway and Bedford New College, University of London.
11 Hall, R. E.: *Ask Any Woman*, Falling Wall Press, Bristol, 1985.
12 *Guardian*, 9 January 1982.
13 BBC Radio 4, *Woman's Hour*, 30 April 1985.
14 *Criminal Statistics for England and Wales*, HMSO, London, 1964 to date.
15 Chambers, G. and Millar, A.: *Investigating Sexual Assault*, Edinburgh, HMSO, 1983.
16 See Chapter 8.
17 *The Sunday Times*, 12 December 1982.
18 Freud, S.: *The Standard Edition of the Complete Psychological Works of Sigmund Freud*, London, Hogarth Press, 1961, Vols III and XIX.
19 Groth, A. N.: *Men who Rape: The Psychology of the Offender*, New York and London, Plenum Press, 1979.
20 Levine, S. and Koenig, J. (eds): *Why Men Rape*, London, W.H. Allen, 1982. p. 50.
21 Amir, M.: *Patterns in Forcible Rape*, Chicago, University of Chicago Press, 1971.
22 Holmstrom, L. L. and Burgess, A. W.: *The Victim of Rape: Institutional Reactions*, New York, John Wiley and Sons, 1978.

23 London Rape Crisis Centre: *Second Report*, London, 1978, p. 8.
24 BBC Radio 4, *Woman's Hour*, 30 April 1985.
25 Ibid.
26 Personal interview.
27 Bohmer, C. and Blumberg, A.: 'Twice traumatized: the rape victim and the court', *Judicature*, vol. 58, no. 8, 1975.
28 Holmstrom, L. L. and Burgess, A. W.: op.cit.
29 Bohmer, C. and Blumberg, A.: op. cit., pp. 398–9.
30 Coote, A. and Gill, T.: *The Rape Controversy*, NCCL, London, 1975, p. 12.
31 *Report of the Advisory Group on the Law of Rape*, HMSO, London, 1975, paras 12–13.
32 R v Henry and Manning (1968), 53 Cr.App.R. at 153.
33 Jackson, S.: 'The social context of rape: sexual scripts and motivation', *Women's Studies International Quarterly*, vol. 1, no. 1, 1978.
34 Berger, V.: 'Man's trial, woman's tribulation: rape cases in the courtroom', *Columbia Law Review*, vol. 77, no. 1, 1977, p. 3.

2 The legal origins

1 Sexual Offences Act 1985.
2 Pollock, F. and Maitland, F. W.: *The History of English Law before the Time of Edward I*, Cambridge, Cambridge University Press, 1898, p. 490.
3 Blackstone, W.: *Commentaries on the Laws of England*, Oxford, Clarendon Press, 1775.
4 Ibid.
5 *Britton on the Laws of England*, translated by F. M. Nichols, Oxford, Clarendon Press, 1865.
6 Brownmiller, S.: *Against Our Will: Men, Women and Rape*, London, Secker and Warburg, 1975.
7 For example, *Kenny's Outlines of Criminal Law*, edited by J. W. Cecil Turner, Cambridge, Cambridge University Press, 19th edn, 1966.
8 *Report of the Advisory Group on the Law of Rape*, London, HMSO, 1975, para. 18.
9 Geis, G.: 'Lord Hale, witches and rape', *British Journal of Law and Society*, vol. 5, no. 1, 1978, p. 26.
10 Hale, M.: *Historia Placitorum Coronae*, London, Nutt and Gosling, 1736, vol 1, p. 629.
11 Gordon, G.: *The Criminal Law of Scotland*, Edinburgh, W. Green, 1967, p. 831.
12 Clive, E. and Wilson, J.: *The Law of Husband and Wife in Scotland*, Edinburgh, W. Green, 1974, p. 376.
13 R v Barker (1829) 3 C&P 589; R v Tissington (1843) 1 Cox 48; R v Greatbanks (1959) Crim.L.R. 450.
14 R v Clarke (1817) 2 Stark 241; R v Clay (1851) 5 Cox 146; R v Riley (1887) 18 QBD 481.
15 R v Hodgson (1812) R&R 211 CCR.
16 Toner, B.: *The Facts of Rape*, London, Arrow, 1982, p. 100.

17 H. C. Debates, vol. 905, col. 802, 1976.
18 Hale, M.: op. cit., 1736, vol. 1, p. 635.
19 Legrand, C. E.: 'Rape and rape laws: sexism in society and law', *California Law Review*, vol. 61, no. 3, 1973; Robin, G. D.: 'Forcible rape: institutionalised sexism in the criminal justice system', *Crime Delinquency*, vol. 23, no. 2, 1977.
20 Hale, M.: op.cit., 1736, vol. 1, p. 633.
21 *Gradwohl's Legal Medicine*, 2nd edn, edited by F. Camps, Bristol, J. Wright and Sons, 1968.
22 Simpson, K.: *A Doctor's Guide to Court*, London, Butterworths, 1962, p. 125.
23 Smith, S. and Fiddes, F. S.: *Forensic Medicine*, London, Churchill, 1955, p. 297.
24 Ibid., p. 299.
25 Chambers, G. and Millar, A.: *Investigating Sexual Assault*, Edinburgh, HMSO, 1983.
26 *Daily Mail*, 17 June 1985.
27 Blair, I.: *Investigating Rape – A New Approach for Police*, London, Croom Helm, 1985, p. 54.
28 Report of a Howard League Working Party: *Unlawful Sex*, London, Waterlow, Legal and Social Policy Library, 1985.
29 Stewart, C. H.: 'A retrospective survey of alleged sexual assault cases', *Police Surgeon*, 1981, pp. 28–32.
30 MacLean, N. M.: 'Rape and false accusations of rape', *Police Surgeon*, 1979, pp. 29–40.
31 Report of the New York Sex Crimes Analysis Unit, quoted in Pattullo, P.: *Judging Women*, London, NCCL, 1983.
32 DPP v Smith (1961) AC 290; Hyam v DPP (1975) AC 55.
33 For a more recent position on this general point, see R v Moloney (1985) 1 All.E. R. 1025.
34 DPP v Morgan and others (1975) 61 Cr.App.R., p. 150.
35 Ibid., p. 166.
36 Ibid., p. 156.
37 Coote, A. and Gill, T.: *The Rape Controversy*, London, National Council for Civil Liberties, 1975; and 'Diogenes on law', *New Society*, vol. 32, no. 657, 1975.
38 The confusion surrounding the matter of criminal intent is further acknowledged and discussed in the Law Commission's 1978 Report on the Mental Element in Crime.
39 *Sunday Mirror*, 4 May 1975.
40 Ibid.
41 Letter to *The Times*, 8 May 1975.
42 H. C. Debates, vol. 892, cols. 1411–18, 1975.
43 *Report on the Advisory Group on the Law of Rape*, op.cit., para. 2.
44 Editorial, *New Society*, vol. 32, no. 664, 1975.
45 *New Law Journal*, vol. 125, no. 5705, 1975, p. 610.
46 Sutherland, E. H.: 'The diffusion of sexual psychopath laws' *American Journal of Sociology*, vol. 56, no. 2, 1950.
47 'Freedom farewell', *New Society*, vol. 31, no. 644, 1975, p. 308.

48 Chibnall, S.: *Law and Order News*, London, Tavistock, 1977.
49 Soothill, K. and Jack, A.: 'How rape is reported', *New Society*, vol. 32, no. 663, 1975.
50 *The Times*, 7 December 1985.
51 Coote, A. and Gill, T.: op.cit., 1975, p. 28.
52 H. C. Debates, vol. 878, col.498, 1974.
53 Report of the Advisory Group on the Law of Rape, op. cit., para. 131.
54 Ibid. para. 137.
55 *The Times*, 11 December 1975.
56 Martin, A.: *New Society*, vol. 34, 18 December 1975, p. 651.
57 *Daily Mail*, 11 December 1975.
58 H. C. Debates, vol. 905, col. 845, 1976.
59 H. C. Debates, vol. 905, col. 845; and vol. 911, col, 1930, 1976.
60 H. C. Debates, vol. 911, col. 1993, 1976.
61 H. C. Debates, vol. 911, col. 2002, 1976.
62 H. C. Debates, vol. 911, col. 1988, 1976.
63 H. C. Debates, vol. 905, col. 807, 1976.
64 The case of R v Viola in 1982 established that it was judgment rather than discretion that was involved in judges' decision-making in this area. The implications of this case are discussed in Chapter 10. However, at the time of the study reported here, this refinement had not been introduced.
65 Geis, G. and Geis, R.: 'Anonymity in rape cases', *Justice of the Peace*, vol. 141, p. 293, 21 May 1977.

3   Rape cases at the Old Bailey

1 Pattullo, P.: *Judging Women*, London, NCCL, 1983, p. 6.
2 Criminal Law Revision Committee: *Fifteenth Report on Sexual Offences*, London, HMSO, 1984.
3 Holmstrom, L. L. and Burgess, A. W.: *The Victim of Rape – Institutional Reactions*, New York, Wiley and Sons, 1978, p. 247.
4 Sanders, W. B.: *Rape and Woman's Identity*, Beverley Hills, Sage Publications, 1980, p. 61.
5 Wright, R.: 'The English rapist', *New Society*, 17 July 1980, p. 124.
6 London Rape Crisis Centre: *Second Report*, London, 1978, p. 6.
7 Barnard, D.: *The Criminal Court in Action*, London, Butterworths, 1974, p. 80.
8 At the time of this study, accused persons had a right to make an unsworn statement from the dock, without having to submit to cross-examination. Section 7 of the Criminal Justice Act 1982 abolished that right: if the defendant chooses to say anything, he must do so on oath and be liable to cross-examination. This provision, had it been in force when this research was being carried out, would have affected only one defendant in the study.
9 Chambers, G. and Millar, A.: *Investigating Sexual Assault*, Edinburgh, HMSO, 1983, p. 76.
10 Quoted in Berger, V.: 'Man's trial, woman's tribulation: rape cases in the courtroom', *Columbia Law Review*, 1977, vol. 77, no. 1, p. 26.

4 The limits of anonymity

1 Soothill, K. and Jack, A.: 'How rape is reported', *New Society*, 19 June 1975.
2 *Report of the Advisory Group on the Law of Rape*, London, HMSO, 1975, para. 153.
3 Geis, G. and Geis, R.: 'Anonymity in rape cases', *Justice of the Peace*, 21 May 1977, p. 293.
4 Criminal Law Revision Committee: *Fifteenth Report on Sexual Offences*, London, HMSO, 1984, para. 2.94.
5 Personal interview.
6 Sexual Offences (Amendment) Act 1976, s.4(2).
7 Sexual Offences (Amendment) Act 1976, s.4(4).
8 *The Times*, 7 February 1978.
9 The *Observer*, 9 September 1984.
10 Personal communication with the Press Council.
11 Hay, A., Soothill, K. and Walby, S.: 'Seducing the country by rape reports', *New Society*, 31 July 1980, p. 214.
12 London Rape Crisis Centre: *Third Report*, London, 1982, p. 16.
13 Hay, A., Soothill, K. and Walby, S.: *op.cit.*, p. 215.
14 H. C. Debates, vol. 911, col. 1927, 1976.
15 H. C. Debates, vol. 911, col. 1926, 1976.
16 Geis, G. and Geis, R.: *op. cit*, p. 293.
17 *Western Daily Press*, 1 March 1980.
18 *Justice of the Peace*, 26 January 1980, p. 47.

5 As his Lordship pleases

1 R v Clarke (1817) 2 Stark at 244.
2 R v Barker (1829) 3 C&P 589.
3 R v Tissington (1843) 1 Cox 48.
4 R v Clay and another (1851) 5 Cox 146.
5 R v Greatbanks (1959) Crim.L.R. 450.
6 R v Hodgson (1812) Russ & Ry 211.
7 Smith, J. C.: 'The Heilbron Report', *Criminal Law Review*, 1976, p. 102.
8 R v Fenlon and others (1980) 71 Cr.App.R. 307.
9 H. C. Debates, vol. 905, col. 850, 1976.
10 R v Lawrence and another (1977) Crim.L.R. 493.
11 *Report of the Advisory Group on the Law of Rape*, London, HMSO, 1975, para. 107.
12 R v Rahimipour (1979) Court of Appeal, Criminal Division 2916/B/78.

6 The importance of being perfect

1 R v Aspinall (1827) cor. Hullock, B. York Spring Assizes, cited in *Stark on Evidence*, 3rd edn, 1842, vol. iii, p. 952.
2 R v Riley (1887) 18 QBD 481.
3 Sanders, W. B.: *Rape and Woman's Identity*, Beverley Hills, Sage

Publications, 1980, p. 26.
4 Holmstrom, L. L. and Burgess, A. W.: *The Victim of Rape – Institutional Reactions*, New York, John Wiley and Sons, 1978, p. 177.
5 Boumelha, P.: *Thomas Hardy and Women: Sexual Ideology and Narrative Form*, Brighton, Harvester Press, 1982, p. 11.
6 Kalven, H. and Zeisel, H.: *The American Jury*, Chicago and London, University of Chicago Press, 1971, p. 249.

7 The prime suspect

1 The category of 'markedly discredited' was rigorously defined and refers to cases where a serious attack was made on the victim's character and where, to some extent at least, the basis of that attack was substantiated by evidence from the prosecution.
2 'Consent to being in the situation' includes all cases where the victim herself agreed that she was in her assailant's company willingly, whether he had 'tricked' her into that situation or not.
3 *Report of the Advisory Group on the Law of Rape*, London, HMSO, 1975, para. 21.
4 Groth, A. N. and Cohen, M. L.: 'Aggressive sexual offenders: diagnosis and treatment', in Burgess, A. W. and Lazare, A.: *Community Mental Health: Target Populations*, Englewood Cliffs, N. J. Prentice Hall, 1976, p. 222.
5 *Halsbury's Laws of England*, 4th edn, vol. II: *Criminal law, Evidence and Procedure*, London, Butterworths, 1976, para. 441, p. 257.
6 Dukes, R. L.: 'Predicting rape victim reportage' *Sociology and Social Research*, vol. 62, no. 1, 1978.
7 Chambers, G. and Millar, A.: *Investigating Sexual Assault*, Edinburgh, HMSO, 1983.
8 Home Office Circular, Ref. POL/82 1098/51/14, dated 18 March 1983.

8 Verdict, mitigation and sentence

1 See Figure 3.1, Chapter 3.
2 The Sexual Offences Act 1985 increased the maximum penalty for indecent assault against a female to ten years' imprisonment.
3 R v Roberts (1982) 4 Cr.App.R (S) 8.
4 R v Taylor (1983) 5 Cr.App.R(S) 241.
5 *Guardian*, 19 November 1985.
6 Thomas, D.: *Principles of Sentencing*, 2nd edn, London, Heinemann, 1979.
7 See Chapter 1.
8 R v Hay (1982) 4 Cr.App.R. (S) 392.
9 R v Docherty (1975) 10/5/C/75.
10 R v Grant (1982) 4 Cr.App.R. (S) 12.
11 R v Cawser (1980) 2 Cr.App.R. (S) 31.
12 R v Owen (1980) 2 Cr.App.R. (S) 45.
13 R v Holmes (1979) 1 Cr.App.R. (S) 233.

14 R v Spence (1982) 4 Cr.App.R. (S).
15 R v Tatum (1980) 2 Cr.App.R. (S) 48.
16 R v Biggs (1979) 1 Cr.App.R. (S) 30.
17 R v Stockwell (1984) 6 Cr.App.R. (S) 84.
18 R v Reeves (1983) 5 Cr.App.R. (S) 188.
19 Thomas, D.: op.cit.
20 R v Galloway (1979) 1 Cr.App.R. (S).
21 R v Buckley (1981) 3 Cr.App.R. (S) 209.
22 R v Rickards (1981) 3 Cr.App.R. (S) 132.
23 R v Roper (1979) 1 Cr.App.R. (S) 303.
24 R v Allcott (1981) 3 Cr.App.R. (S) 18.
25 R v Lionel (1982) 4 Cr.App.R. (S).

9 The lesson from abroad

1 Texas Penal Code Ann.tit.5, Para. 21.13(a) 1976–7.
2 New York Crim. Proc. Law, Para. 60.42(5) 1976–7.
3 Berger, V.: 'Man's trial, woman's tribulation: rape cases in the courtroom', *Columbia Law Review*, vol. 77, no. 1, 1977, p. 39.
4 Evidence Act Amendment Act 1976 (No. 84) of South Australia, s.34i.
5 Evidence Act Amendment Act 1976 (No.145) of Western Australia.
6 Criminal Law (Sexual Offences) Act 1978 of Queensland.
7 Crimes (Sexual Assault) Amendment Act 1981 of New South Wales.
8 Borgida, E. and White, P.: 'Social perception of rape victims – the impact of legal reform', *Law and Human Behaviour*, vol. 2, no. 4, 1978, p. 349.
9 Cited in the Australian Law Reform Commission's Research Paper II, Character and conduct, 1982.
10 R v Gun (1977) 17 S.A.S.R.
11 Ibid.
12 Temkin, J.: 'Regulating sexual history evidence – the limits of discretionary legislation', 33 *I.C.L.Q.*, 1984a.
13 R v Gun (1977) 17 S.A.S.R.
14 O'Connor, D.: 'Rape law reform – the Australian experience' (Part 2), *Criminal Law Journal*, vol. 2, 1978.
15 Woods, G. D.: *Sexual Assault Law Reforms in New South Wales – A Commentary on the Crimes (Sexual Assault) Amendment Act 1982 and Cognate Act*, Department of Attorney General and of Justice, 1981, p. 31.
16 Scutt, J. A. (ed.): *Rape Law Reform*, Australian Institute of Criminology, Canberra, 1980.
17 Newby, L.: 'Rape victims in court: the Western Australian example', in Scutt, J.A. (ed.): op.cit.
18 M.C.L.A. 750.520a and following.
19 Nordby, V. B.: 'Reforming rape laws: the Michigan experience', in Scutt, J. A. (ed.): op.cit., p. 6.
20 Ibid., p. 21.
21 Marsh, J. C., Geist, A. and Caplan, N.: *Rape and the Limit of Law Reform*, Auburn House Publishing Co., 1982.

22 Berger, V.: op.cit., p. 71.
23 Scottish Law Commission: *Evidence – Report on Evidence in Cases of Rape and other Sexual Offences*, Paper no. 78, Edinburgh, HMSO, 1983, para. 5.2.
24 Ibid.
25 Newby, L.: op.cit., p. 121.
26 Honoré, T.: *Sex Law*, London, Duckworth, 1978, p. 66.
27 Criminal Law Revision Committee: *Fifteenth Report on Sexual Offences*, HMSO, London, 1984, para. 2.87.
28 Ibid., para. 2.88.
29 Ibid., para. 2.89.

10   An insoluble problem?

1 There has been a good deal of rather technical legal discussion of the decision in DPP v Morgan and its implications for the concept of intent in rape. The main issues are discussed by J. Temkin in an article entitled 'The limits of reckless rape', *Criminal Law Review*, 1983. There exist a number of judgments subsequent to Morgan on the concept of recklessness – the reader may wish to consult R v Caldwell (1981) 1 All.E.R. 961; and R v Pigg (1982) 74 Cr.App.R. 352, CA.
2 London Weekend Television, *Weekend World* Programme, 14 February 1982.
3 *Report of the Advisory Group on the Law of Rape*, London, HMSO, 1975, para. 131.
4 Elliott, D.W.: 'Rape complainants' sexual experience with third parties', *Criminal Law Review*, 1984.
5 R v Viola (1982) 75 Cr.App.R. 125.
6 Criminal Law Revision Committee: *Fifteenth Report on Sexual Offences*, London, HMSO, 1984, para. 2.90.
7 Mitra, C.: ' . . . For she has no right or power to refuse her consent', *Criminal Law Review*, 1979, p. 561.
8 For a detailed discussion of these issues, see Criminal Law Revision Committee: op.cit., 1984, paras. 2.55–2.85.
9 Criminal Law Revision Committee: op.cit., 1984, para. 2.73.
10 Ibid., para. 2.69.
11 Criminal Law Revision Committee: *Working Paper on Sexual Offences*, London, HMSO, 1980, para. 42.
12 Legrand, C.E.: 'Rape and rape laws – sexism in society and law', *California Law Review*, vol. 61, 1973, p. 926.
13 Williams, J.: 'Marital rape – time for reform', *New Law Journal*, vol. 134, no. 6137, 1984, p. 27.
14 Advisory Group on the Law of Rape: op.cit., para. 80.
15 Card, R.: 'The Criminal Law Revision Committee's Working Paper on Sexual Offences', *Criminal Law Review*, 1981, p. 373.
16 R v Rai (1982) Leeds Crown Court.
17 Temkin, J.: 'Towards a modern law of rape', 45, *Modern Law Review*, 1982,

p. 412.

18 Benn, M., Coote, A. and Gill, T.: *The Rape Controversy*, NCCL, London, 1983, p. 26.

19 Criminal Law Revision Committee: op.cit., 1980, para. 49.

20 Woods, G. D.: *Sexual Assault Law Reforms in New South Wales – A Commentary on the Crimes (Sexual Assault) Amendment Act 1981 and Cognate Act*, Department of Attorney-General and of Justice, 1981, p. 28.

21 Pattullo, P.: *Judging Women*, London, NCCL, 1983, p. 37.

22 H. C. Debates, vol. 917, col. 886, 15 October 1976.

23 Wood, P. L.: 'The victim in a forcible rape case: a feminist view', *American Criminal Law Review*, 1973, p. 354.

Select bibliography

Abrahamsen, D.: *The Psychology of Crime*, New York, John Wiley and Sons, 1960.

Adler Z.: 'Rape: the intention of Parliament and the practice of the courts', *Modern Law Review*, 1982.

Adler Z.: 'The relevance of sexual history evidence in rape: problems of subjective interpretation', *Criminal Law Review*, 1985.

Amir, M.: *Patterns in Forcible Rape*, Chicago, University of Chicago Press, 1971.

Arabian, A.: 'The cautionary instruction in sex cases: a lingering insult', *Southwestern University Law Review*, 1978.

Archbold on Pleading, Evidence and Practice in Criminal Cases, 39th edn, edited by Mitchell, S., London, Sweet and Maxwell, 1976.

Barnard, D.: *The Criminal Court in Action*, London, Butterworths, 1974.

Benn, M., Coote, A. and Gill, T.: *The Rape Controversy*, London, NCCL, 1983.

Berger, V.: 'Man's trial, woman's tribulation: rape cases in the courtroom', *Columbia Law Review*, 1977.

Bienen, L.: 'Rape II: the rape laws of fifty states', *Women's Rights Law Reporter*, 1977.

Blair, I.: *Investigating Rape – A New Approach for Police*, London, Croom Helm, 1985.

Blom-Cooper, L. and Drewry, G.: *Law and Morality*, London, Duckworth, 1975.

Bohmer, C.: 'Judicial attitudes towards rape victims', *Judicature*, 1975.

Bohmer, C. and Blumberg, A.: 'Twice traumatized: the rape victim and the court', *Judicature*, 1975.

Borgida, E. and White, P.: 'Social perception of rape victims – the impact of legal reform', *Law and Human Behaviour*, 1978.

Bowker, L. H.: *Women and Crime in America*, Macmillan, New York, 1981.

Brodyaga, L. et al.: *Rape and its Victims: A Report for Citizens*, Washington D. C., Health Facilities and Criminal Justice Agencies, Center for Women's Policy Studies, 1975.

Brooks, N.: 'Rape and the laws of evidence', *Chitty's Law Journal*, 1975.

Brownmiller, S.: *Against Our Will: Men, Women and Rape*, London, Secker and Warburg, 1975.

Burgess, A. W. and Holmstrom, L. L.: *Rape – Crisis and Recovery*, Bowie, Maryland, R. J. Brady Co., 1979.

Select bibliography

Bush, J. P.: *Rape in Australia*, Melbourne, Sun Books, 1977.

Card, R.: 'The Criminal Law Revision Committee's Working Paper on Sexual Offences', *Criminal Law Review*, 1981.

Chambers, G. and Millar, A.: *Investigating Sexual Assault*, Edinburgh, HMSO, 1983.

Chappell, D.: 'Cross-cultural research on forcible rape', *International Journal of Criminology and Penology*, 1976.

Clark, L. and Lewis, D.: *Rape: The Price of Coercive Sexuality*, Toronto, Toronto Women's Press, 1977.

Cohen, M. D.: 'Evidence of the complainant's previous sexual conduct in a rape trial', *New Law Journal*, 1980.

Criminal Law Revision Committee: *Working Paper on Sexual Offences*, London, HMSO, 1980.

Criminal Law Revision Committee: *Fifteenth Report on Sexual Offences*, London, HMSO, 1984.

Criminal Statistics for England and Wales, London, HMSO, 1964 to 1984.

Cross on Evidence, 6th edn, ed. C. Tapper, London, Butterworths, 1985.

Davidson, T.: *Conjugal Crime*, New York, Ballantine Books, 1978.

Deming, M. B. and Eppy, A.: 'The sociology of rape', *Sociology and Social Research*, 1981.

Dobash, R. E. and Dobash, R.: *Violence against Wives: A Case against the Patriarchy*, London, Open Books, 1980.

Drapkin, I. and Viano, E (eds): *Victimology*, Lexington, Mass., D. C. Heath, 1974.

Dukes, R. L.: 'Predicting rape victim reportage', *Sociology and Social Research*, 1978.

Edwards, S.: 'Sex crimes in the 19th century', *New Society*, 1979.

Edwards, S.: *Female Sexuality and the Law*, London, Martin Robertson, 1981.

Edwards, S.: 'Rape: a consideration of "contributory negligence", the mandatory sentence, and police procedures', *Justice of the Peace*, 1982.

Eisenberg, R. L.: 'Abolishing cautionary instructions in sex offence cases' *Criminal Law Bulletin*, 1976.

Elliott, D. W.: 'Rape complainants' sexual experience with third parties,' *Criminal Law Review*, 1984.

Findlay, B. 'The cultural context of rape', *Women Lawyers' Journal*, 1974.

Freeman, M. D. A.: 'But if you can't rape your wife, whom can you rape?' *Family Law Quarterly*, 1981.

Freud, S.: *The Standard Edition of the Complete Psychological Works of Sigmund Freud*, London, Hogarth Press, 1961.

Gager, N. and Schurr, C.: *Sexual Assault: Confronting Rape in America*, New York, Grosset and Dunlap, 1976.

Gagnon, J. H. and Simon, W.: *Sexual Conduct*, London, Hutchinson, 1974.

Geis, G.: 'Lord Hale, witches and rape', *British Journal of Law and Society*, 1978.

Geis, G. and Geis R. (eds): *Forcible Rape*, New York, Columbia University Press, 1977.

Geis, G. and Geis, R: 'Rape reform: an appreciative-critical review', *Bulletin of the American Academy of Psychiatry and Law*, 1978.

Select bibliography

Gilley, J.: 'How to help the raped', *New Society*, 1974.

Griffin, S.: 'Rape – the all-American crime', *Ramparts*, 1971.

Groth, A. N.: *Men who Rape: The Psychology of the Offender*, New York and London, Plenum Press, 1979.

Haines, E. C.: 'The character of the rape victim', *Chitty's Law Journal*, 1975.

Hale, M.: *Historia Placitorum Coronae*, London, Nutt and Gosling, 1736.

Hall, R., James, S. and Kertesz, J.: *The Rapist who Pays the Rent: Women's Case for Changing the Law on Rape*, Falling Wall Press, Bristol, 1984.

Hanmer, J. and Saunders, S.: *Well-founded Fear*, Hutchinson, London, 1984.

Harper, R. and McWhinnie, A.: *The Glasgow Rape Case*, Hutchinson, London, 1983.

Hay, A., Soothill, K. and Walby, S.: 'Seducing the country by rape reports' *New Society*, 1980.

Hibey, R. A.: 'The trial of a rape case: an advocate's analysis of corroboration, consent and character', *American Law Review*, 1973.

Hilberman, E.: *The Rape Victim*, Washington D. D., American Psychiatric Association, 1976.

Holmstrom, L. L. and Burgess, A. W.: *The Victim of Rape: Institutional Reactions*, New York, John Wiley and Sons, 1978.

Honoré, T.: *Sex Law*, London, Duckworth, 1978.

Horos, C. V.: *Rape*, New Canaan, Conn., Tobey Publishing Co., 1974.

Hough, M. and Mayhew, P.: *The British Crime Survey: First Report*, London, HMSO, 1983.

Jackson, S.: 'The social context of rape: sexual scripts and motivation', *Women's Studies International Quarterly*, 1978.

Jones, C. and Aronson, E.: 'Attribution of fault to a rape victim as a function of the respectability of the victim', *Journal of Personality and Social Psychology*, 1974.

Kalven, H. and Zeisel, H.: *The American Jury*, Chicago and London, University of Chicago Press, 1971.

Katz, S. and Mazur, M. A.: *Understanding the Rape Victim*, New York and Oxford, John Wiley, 1979.

Komisar, L.: *Violence and the Masculine Mystique*, (pamphlet), Pittsburgh, Pa. Know Inc., 1971.

Law Commission: *Report on the Mental Element in Crime*, Law Commission No. 89, London, HMSO, 1978.

Legrand, C. E.: 'Rape and rape laws: sexism in society and law', *California Law Review*, 1973.

Levine, S. and Koenig, J. (eds): *Why Men Rape*, London, W. H. Allen, 1982.

Lipsitt, P. D. and Sales, B. D. (eds): *New Directions in Psycholegal Research*, Van Nostrand Reinhold Co., New York, 1980.

London Rape Crisis Centre: *First Report*, 1977; *Second Report*, 1978; *Third Report*, 1982.

London Rape Crisis Centre: *Sexual Violence – The Reality for Women*, The Women's Press, London, 1984.

Luginbill, D. H.: 'Repeal of the corroboration requirement: will it tip the scales of justice?' *Drake Law Review*, 1975.

MacKay, R. D.: 'Some developments in the law of rape', *Justice of the Peace*,

Select bibliography

1982.

Marsh, J. C., Geist, A. and Caplan, N.: *Rape and the Limit of Law Reform*, Auburn House Publishing Co., 1982.

Mazelan, P. M.: 'Stereotypes and perceptions of the victims of rape', *Victimology*, 1980.

McNamara, P.: 'Cross-examination of the complainant in a trial for rape', *Criminal Law Journal*, 1981.

Medea, A. and Thompson, K.: *Against Rape*, New York, Farrar, Strauss and Giroux, 1974.

Mitra, C.: ' . . . For she has no right or power to refuse her consent', *Criminal Law Review*, 1979.

Mukherjee, S. K. and Scutt, J. A. (eds): *Women and Crime*, Sydney, Allen and Unwin, 1981.

National Legal Data Center: *Rape Legislation: A Digest of its History and Current Legal Status*, Seattle, Washington, Battelle Law and Justice Study Center, 1975.

New South Wales Department of the Attorney General and of Justice, Criminal Law Review Division: *Report on Rape and Various Other Sexual Offences*, 1977.

Notman, M. T. and Nadelson, C. C.: 'The rape victim: psychodynamic considerations', *American Journal of Psychiatry*, 1976.

O'Connor, D.: 'Rape law reform – the Australian experience' (Part 2), *Criminal Law Journal*, 1978.

Pattullo, P.: *Judging Women*, London, NCCL, 1983.

Pickard, T.: 'Culpable mistakes and rape: relating mens rea to the crime', *University of Toronto Law Journal*, 1980.

Polak, A. L.: 'Can a husband be found guilty of raping his wife?' *Justice of the Peace*, 1979.

Reeves Sanday, P.: 'The social context of rape', *New Society*, 1982.

Report of a Howard League Working Party: *Unlawful Sex*, London, Waterlow Legal and Social Policy Library, 1985.

Report of the Advisory Group on the Law of Rape, London, HMSO, 1975.

Reynolds, J.: 'Rape as social control', *Catalyst*, 1974.

Robin, G. D.: 'Forcible rape: institutionalised sexism in the criminal justice system', *Crime and Delinquency*, 1977.

Rose, V.: 'Rape as a social problem: a by-product of the feminist movement', *Social Problems*, 1977.

Russell, D. E. H.: *Rape in Marriage*, New York, Macmillan, 1982.

Sanders, W. B.: *Rape and Woman's Identity*, Beverley Hills, Sage Publications, 1980.

Schurr, C.: *Rape: Victim as Criminal*, (pamphlet), Pittsburgh, Pa., Know Inc., 1971.

Schwendinger, J. R. and Schwendinger, H.: 'Rape myths in legal, theoretical and everyday practice', *Crime and Social Justice*, 1974.

Schwendinger, J. R. and Schwendinger, H.: 'A review of rape literature', *Crime and Social Justice*, 1976.

Scottish Law Commission: *Evidence – Report on Evidence in Cases of Rape and Other Sexual Offences*, Paper no. 78, Edinburgh, HMSO, 1983.

Select bibliography

Scutt, J. A.: 'Fraud and consent in rape: comprehension of the nature and character of the act and its moral implications', *Criminal Law Quarterly*, 1976.

Scutt, J. A.: 'Admissibility of sexual history evidence and allegations in rape cases', *Australian Law Journal*, 1979.

Scutt, J. A. (ed): *Rape Law Reform*, Australian Institute of Criminology, Canberra, 1980.

Silverman, R. A.: 'Victim precipitation: an examination of the concept', in Drapkin, I. and Viano, E. C. (eds): *Victimology: A New Focus*, vol. 1, Lexington, Mass., Lexington Books, 1974.

Smart, C. and Smart, B. (eds): *Women, Sexuality and Social Control*, Routledge & Kegan Paul, London, 1978.

Smith, J. C.: 'The Heilbron Report', *Criminal Law Review*, 1976.

Soothill, K., Gibbens, T. C. N. and Jack, A.: 'Rape: a 22 year cohort study', *Medicine, Science and the Law*, 1976.

Soothill, K. and Jack, A.: 'How rape is reported', *New Society*, 1975.

Soothill, K., Way, C. and Gibbens, T. C. N.: 'Rape acquittals', *Modern Law Review*, 1980.

Sutherland, S. and Scherl, D. J.: 'Patterns of response among victims of rape', *American Journal of Orthopsychiatry*, 1970.

Telling, D.: 'Rape – consent and belief', *Journal of Criminal Law*, 1983.

Temkin, J.: 'Towards a modern law of rape', *Modern Law Review*, 1982.

Temkin, J.: 'The limits of reckless rape', *Criminal Law Review*, 1983.

Temkin, J.: 'Regulating sexual history evidence – the limits of discretionary legislation', *I.C.L.Q.*, 1984a.

Temkin, J.: 'Evidence in sexual assault cases: the Scottish proposal and alternatives to it', *Modern Law Review*, 1984b.

Toner, B.: *The Facts of Rape*, London, Arrow, 1982.

Viano, E. C. (ed.): *Victims and Society*, Washington D. C., Visage Press, 1976.

Wells, C.: 'Law reform, rape and ideology', *Journal of Law and Society*, 1985.

Williams, G.: 'Corroboration in sexual cases', *Criminal Law Review*, 1962.

Williams, J.: 'Marital rape – time for reform', *New Law Journal*, 1984.

Wood, P. L.: 'The victim in a forcible rape case: a feminist view', *American Criminal Law Review*, 1973.

Wright, R.: 'The English rapist', *New Society*, 17 July 1980.

Index

193

Index

Index

For Product Safety Concerns and Information please contact our EU
representative GPSR@taylorandfrancis.com
Taylor & Francis Verlag GmbH, Kaufingerstraße 24, 80331 München, Germany